D1528858

Dear Teen: WE'RE IN THIS TOGETHER

Let God lead,

Macy Gerig

Dear Teen: We're In This Together
© Macy Gerig

All rights reserved.

ISBN 9798717321709
Wauseon, OH

Printed in the United States of America

To every teen
seeking direction

Table of Contents

7
INTRODUCTION

9
FORGIVEN AND FREE

13
STANDING FIRM IN YOUR IDENTITY

21
ENDURING WITH FAITH

29
FRIENDSHIPS

33
TOXIC FRIENDSHIPS

39
HEALING FROM BROKEN FRIENDSHIPS

45
GODLY FRIENDSHIPS

53
THE RESPONSIBILITIES OF A GOOD FRIEND

57
DATING RELATIONSHIPS

63
LEARNING FROM PAST DATING RELATIONSHIPS

77
WAITING FOR GOD'S TIMING

83
GODLY DATING

91
FINDING TIME WITH JESUS

99
LIVING OUT YOUR FAITH

107
MY TESTIMONY

115
ACKNOWLEDGEMENTS

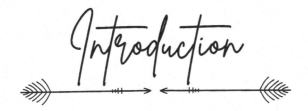

Introduction

Welcome! I am so overjoyed that God put this book in your hands to read! Let me start by introducing myself: I'm Macy. An extremely outgoing girl who loves coffee, friends and family, church, shopping trips, traveling, working out, music, and sports (specifically soccer and dive). I go to school and live pretty much like any other high school teenager. But wait, there's something different about me. I'm a total Jesus girl who accepted Jesus into my life at a young age and strives to live in a way that brings glory back to Him through every decision, friendship, relationship, and circumstance I'm put in. I know, speaking from personal experience, friend situations can be toxic, relationships can get sticky and emotional, finding time with Jesus can be a puzzle due to schedules and calendars, living out your faith can be scary, and embracing your God-given identity can be a challenge!

I am nowhere close to perfect. I don't have everything figured out, and I certainly don't know everything about God. However, I believe God can use you to do incredible things when you are obedient to His will. I believe God will show you his love and mercy through Jesus when you ask. And when you surrender, I know God can (and will) forgive your past mistakes as He welcomes you into an eternal relationship with Him. Now it's up to you to take that step of entrusting your whole life to Jesus.

The chapters in this book are divided into topics that I have witnessed and personally experienced throughout my teenage years. I pray that God speaks to your heart throughout these chapters. I pray that this book guides and navigates you through finding your God-given identity, standing firm in your faith, navigating godly friendships and relationships, spending time with Jesus, and living out your faith. I pray God uses it to strengthen your walk with Him in a way that allows you to stand firm in the path God has set out for you. Now that you have an idea of who I am and what this book entails, let's dive into the first chapter, "Forgiven and Free."

FORGIVEN AND FREE

One of the most common things I've heard from teenagers is, "God won't forgive me for the things I've done," or, "I want to have a better relationship with God, but I've made too many mistakes." Just typing that line makes my heart hurt. I am saddened that we are so prone to believe such lies! So many people believe that they've crossed too many lines, said too many words, or detoured through the wrong path one too many times to be loved and accepted by God. Before getting too far into this book, you have to understand who God is and what He did for you in order to begin a relationship with Him. Once you understand that, every topic and chapter in the book follows because of your commitment to living for God.

Teenagers believe that their mistakes are unforgivable because they have a misinterpretation of who God truly is. God doesn't hold your mistakes against you. He will not shame or guilt you because you forgot to switch the laundry around like your parents asked. Even better, He isn't turning His back on you because you aren't perfect. In fact, God knows we aren't perfect and continues to give us love and grace. In order to begin a relationship with Him, you have to understand who God is.

Who our God is:
  o Faithful (1 Corinthians 10:13)

- o Patient (2 Peter 3:9)
- o Gracious and merciful (Hebrews 4:16)
- o Provider (Matthew 6:33)
- o Righteous and compassionate (Psalms 116:5)
- o Protector (2 Thessalonians 3:3)
- o Savior (John 3:16)

The list could continue. The point is, our God is good. He is wonderful and He loves you unconditionally. Does that sound like someone who wouldn't forgive you? Does that sound like someone who would turn His back on you due to a mistake? Absolutely not. In fact, God sent His Son to die for you so your sins could be buried. He loves you - yes you - so much that He wanted to break the power that sin had in your life. In Romans 5:6-9, the Apostle Paul wrote, "When we were utterly helpless, Christ came at just the right time and died for us sinners. Now, most people would not be willing to die for an upright person, though someone might perhaps be willing to die for a person who is especially good. But God showed his great love for us by sending Christ to die for us while we were still sinners. And since we have been made right in God's sight by the blood of Christ, he will certainly save us from God's condemnation" (NLT)(9).

"OUR GOD IS GOOD. HE IS WONDERFUL AND HE LOVES YOU."

This might be confusing at first, but let me try to explain this further. Before Jesus died on the cross, we (humans) were judged by the law. The law consists of the Ten Commandments; don't lie, steal, cheat, dishonor your parents, accuse, or idolize worldly things. However, no human could live up to that unattainable expectation because we were born with a sinful nature.

Our sinful nature draws us away from God. From the beginning, God created us to have a relationship with Him. In order to assure that we could have a relationship with Him forever, He sent His son, Jesus, to be born as a baby and die as our Savior. Jesus died for our sins on the cross, so that we could have eternal life in Heaven with God. Once Jesus had died, he was buried in a tomb for three days. On the third day, Mary Magdalene (one of Jesus's followers) went to Jesus' tomb. When she arrived at the tomb, an angel appeared and said, " I know you are looking for Jesus, who was crucified. He isn't here! He is risen from the dead, just as he said would happen" (Matthew 28:5-6 NLT) (9). Jesus rose from the dead and beat the power of death.

In the passage I shared from Romans, the Apostle Paul tells us that "... we have been made right in God's sight by the blood of Christ" (NLT) (9). Listen to me very carefully: Jesus already took your sins to the grave. There's no mistake you could make that would force God to not love you. You are loved by God. I get that you might have made some choices that you regret. However, everyone has a past. I mean, today is tomorrow's past, right? I'm just saying, your past doesn't define you. Your mistakes don't have to determine your future. God does. Even if you crossed a physical line in a relationship, lied, cheated, smoked, stole, or worse, God forgives and shows grace towards those who have placed their trust in Him.

Desiring obedience to Jesus is crucial to living a Christ-centered life. Every encouragement and tip in this book starts from a confession and commitment to Jesus. After that, you begin the best part, freedom in Christ! The Bible says that when you confess with your mouth and believe in your heart that Jesus Christ is Lord, you will be saved (Romans 1:9)(9). You will be saved from lies, worries, shameful decisions, fears, and mistakes that you've made. When you truly give your mistakes to Jesus, you can be free knowing your identity isn't in your mistakes anymore. Your identity is in Jesus. Now, people may remind you of your past with hurtful comments. However, you cannot let these comments take away your freedom in Jesus. When people remind you of your past, you have to restate the truth that you are a new creation and remain faithful to building a relationship with God. When you remain faithful to growing in your relationship with God, He will give you all that you need to persevere.

STANDING FIRM IN YOUR IDENTITY

If you're like me, you know that being a teenager who follows Jesus isn't always the most popular identity with peers. It can put you on a roller coaster ride of emotions. You can experience God's amazing power working in your heart one minute, and the next you get a mean message from a kid at your school because you are "too pure" or "too Christian."

Let me tell you right now that being a Christian, in general, is hard. Being a godly teenager is a whole new level of difficulty. Jesus tells us that we will suffer for living according to His purpose. He tells us that we will experience pushback because the world is not fond of Jesus. Since we choose to deny the world's values and take up the cross, we no longer fit into the world's identity for teens. We stand firm in our faith and identify ourselves in Jesus. The Bible tells us this in John 15:18-19: "If the world hates you, remember that it hated me first. The world would love you as one of its own if you belonged to it, but you are no longer part of the world. I chose you to come out of the world, so it hates you" (NLT)(9).

You see, God chose us before we were created in the womb. Jeremiah 1:5 says, "I knew you before I formed you in your mother's womb. Before you were born, I set you apart..." (NLT)(9). God created us to be set apart, to be different, and to live a life that puts Him on display. By living a Godly life, of course, you're going to get comments back. Of course, people are going to think of you differently. Of course, you will be condemned because of your faith. The lifestyle you live isn't what's popular in this world. To "fit in" in this world is to be held captive by sexual sin, lust, greed, popularity, self-love, and worldly desires. Life in Jesus means freedom from these captives and faith to follow Him and to obey His commands.

In order to follow and obey Jesus, there are a few steps you need to take. The first thing you have to do is get your priorities straight. You cannot give yourself both to the world and to Jesus. You have to choose. You have to choose to take up the cross every single day. Choosing to take up the cross every day means choosing to follow and trust Jesus. It means choosing God's desires instead of your own. It means changing your attitude and actions to glorify God. Now don't think if you make a mistake, God will turn His back on you. That's not the case at all. In fact, we will all fall short of the law, however, I told you before, if you've confessed with your mouth and believe in your heart that Jesus Christ is Lord, then He has forgiven and redeemed you. You are free from your mistakes.

If you're a perfectionist, it's easy to think, "If I just do everything perfectly, no one will have anything bad to say about me." That was me. I thought that if I did everything right, no one would have any topic to harass me about, but people found a way to use my lifestyle against me.

If you are someone who suffers from perfectionism, you need to ask yourself, "Who am I trying to be perfect for? Me? My parents? My friends? The world's approval?" Have a vulnerable conversation with yourself. Understand the desire behind the behavior. When I took an honest look at my actions, I realized that I was trying to be perfect for the approval of other people. But the thing was, others didn't expect me to be perfect. In fact, acting like I was perfect only led to others disapproval. Therefore, I wasn't accomplishing the goal behind acting perfectly, and I was fading from my faith.

Following Jesus requires faith and determination. You will get discouraged and taunted, but God will give you the strength to continue. The people that make comments against you are attempting to discourage you from being a light for Christ. I have received many comments about my faith, including...

YOU NEED TO ASK YOURSELF, "WHO AM I TRYING TO BE PERFECT FOR?"

- o "...oh you're a Christian"
- o "Macy won't do that, she's Christian"
- o "Turn that music off, Macy's Christian ears can't hear that"
- o "You post too much about Jesus"
- o "You're just looking for attention"
- o "You're too Christian"
- o "You won't have any fun with us because you're Christian"

I'm not going to lie, some of those comments hurt in the moment. Typing them out makes me sad because I can't believe that I let such little things get to me. The thing is, those people are making fun of the identity they see, but through their worldly lens. Your identity lies in Jesus. If people are making fun of that, then you must be doing something right.

Think about going shopping as a little kid. You go through a thousand stores and you're bored out of your mind, but when you get to that one store, you feel like it was created just for you. Rightfully, you have to pick a favorite shirt and buy it. Now, since it's your new fav, you have to wear it to school. You love that shirt so much that you jump out of bed the morning before school because you are SO excited to wear it. You run into school and just as you get into the classroom a classmate says something like, "Why are you wearing that? What is that; a hand-me-down?" Immediately, your heart drops and you begin to doubt everything you ever thought about wearing it. You might be so ashamed that you wish you could go home, change clothes, and start the day all over again.

Listen, I get I'm talking about a little kid and a shirt but this is a lot like our faith. We have this huge love for Jesus, and we feel like we need to put it on and share it with the world. But as soon as someone makes a negative comment about our love for Jesus, we start to doubt. We start to think negatively about who we are and if what we stand for really matters. We become so concerned that we won't fit in or get invited that we belittle our own faith. The hurt that we feel may take us away from the original excitement that we felt just seconds before.

As Christians, we know that we are different. We know we are God's children. However, because of our faith, our lives must look different. James 1:22 says, "But don't just listen to God's Word. You must do what it says. Otherwise, you are only fooling yourselves" (NLT)(9). That might sound a little harsh, but God doesn't just want our Sunday-selves. God wants us to show our faith by living our life as an example. We shouldn't participate in parties, drunkenness, toxic situations, or sexual immoralities because those are going to take us away from God. We won't participate in the same kind of "fun" that the world has because that's not the lifestyle we are called to live. Living a lifestyle that honors God will result in comments from people. Remember, those comments should never pull you away from your identity in Jesus Christ. Rather, it should give you even more determination to stand firm in your faith. Standing firm might not be easy, but it will be so rewarding it in the end.

You might be thinking, "Macy, how do I stand firm in my faith with comments behind my back? How do I continue to find my identity in Jesus?"

I am so glad you asked! Let's take a little trip to Ephesians 6:10-18.

"A final word: Be strong in the Lord and in his mighty power. Put on all of God's armor so that you will be able to stand firm against all strategies of the devil. For we are not fighting against flesh-and-blood enemies, but against evil rulers and authorities of the unseen world, against mighty powers in this dark world, and against evil spirits in the heavenly places. Therefore, put on every piece of God's armor so you will be able to resist the enemy in the time of evil. Then after the battle, you will still be standing firm. Stand your ground, putting on the belt of truth and the body armor of God's righteousness. For shoes, put on the peace that comes from the Good News so that you will be fully prepared. In addition to all of these, hold up the Truth shield of faith to stop the fiery arrows of the devil. Put on salvation as your helmet, and take the sword of the Spirit, which is the word of God. Pray in the Spirit at all times and on every occasion. Stay alert and be persistent in your prayers for all believers everywhere" (NLT)(9).

Wow. God really does give us our answer. We cannot possibly stand firm by ourselves. I don't care if you can lift one pound or a thousand pounds, you simply aren't strong enough to stand alone when fighting spiritual battles. God doesn't ever mention that we're on our own when fighting to glorify Him. He tells us we must leave it in His hands and allow Him to strengthen us. To do that though, we have to suit up. We have to put on the full armor of God so that we don't lose ourselves in the process.

In order to stand firm in God's armor, we must first put on the "belt of truth." The belt of truth means to cling to the true word of God. There is a lot of noise in this world; noise from social media, peers, music, and public opinion. In the midst of the noise, we can lose God's truth and begin to believe the popular opinion. The enemy uses people's words, actions, distractions, doubts, and concerns to stop us from God's calling in our life; to stop us from believing what we know to be true. The people that come to mock you are really just the enemy trying to stop you. That's why we have to look towards God's word. When reading the Bible, we are filled with the promises and fulfillments of God. That's why when the noise gets loud, we have to get quiet with God and understand that:

- God overcame the world.
- Your battles are not for you to fight alone.
- He loves you and called you to live according to His purpose.
- God has a plan for you.
- Your faithfulness will not go unseen.

Restating His truth allows our minds to rest in His promises. His truth stops the worry and fear that comes from the enemy's lies. His truth allows us to find comfort in knowing our identity isn't in what people say, but in God.

The second step is to put on the peace that comes from the Good News. God gives us peace that surpasses all understanding, meaning it cannot be found through earthly ideas. This peace only comes from the Holy Spirit. We cannot let people's words corrupt the peace that God lavishes upon us. God sent His Son to die for us so that we could be free. He died so we could have peace knowing we would be with Him in heaven one day. He died so that you could have a relationship with Him. He died so that you could see yourself in the same way that God sees you! There's peace in knowing that no matter what is said about you, God's opinion is the only one that matters.

Verse 16 tells us to hold up the shield of faith. Faith is believing in what we can't see. Faith is believing in God's love, goodness, and mercy. Faith is trusting that God's plan is greater when the world is telling you to fear. Faith is whole-heartedly trusting in God's promises. Faith is a weapon that no person can ever take from you. When God says to hold up the shield of faith, He is telling you to use faith to protect your heart and mind from allowing irrational ideas and thoughts to surpass God's promises. When people say things about you or your lifestyle, faith is knowing that God will shield and protect you from those who do you wrong. Faith is choosing to love and show grace to everyone, even if you aren't getting it in return. Faith is also trusting that God has more in store for you when your plan doesn't work or desire isn't fulfilled. Faith is knowing God will take care of you in a broken world.

The final thing said in the passage from Ephesians is that we should use prayer as our main weapon. Prayer is a simple conversation with God. It is the connection between life on earth and eternity in heaven. Through our undeserved salvation, God gave us a direct connection to Him through prayer. When people make you doubt your identity or when people say things that take away your hope, pray about it. Give your battles to the Lord. It's extremely easy to allow yourself to dwell upon things you cannot fix. You can't make someone take back what they said about you. You can't change the horrible things in the world. However, you can give it to the Lord and spare yourself the hurt or worry. Don't take things upon yourself that aren't yours to fight.

WE SHOULD USE PRAYERS AS OUR MAIN WEAPON.

Your identity rests in the Lord. As a teenager, you will find times when comments are made about your faith or about who you are in Jesus

Christ. When things like that come about, stand firm in your faith and put on the full armor of God so that you can find peace in who you are in Jesus Christ. Continue to live your life in a way that represents the cross. If people have a problem with that, it's not a reflection on you. Allow your faith to remain steadfast - don't be the little kid who throws away the new shirt because someone said one thing bashing it. News flash: you're going to get a lot of hate for loving Jesus, and that should be a compliment to who you are and what you're doing. Use the tools from Ephesians 6 to stand up for what you believe in, and always keep your identity in the Lord strong.

ENDURING WITH FAITH

Life can get messy, and this is also true for Christians! Just because we are made new in Christ doesn't mean we won't still face trials. Actually, God tells us we will face suffering, but, luckily enough, we have our faith to endure and persevere during those difficult times.

Have you ever heard the expression, "Why do bad things happen to good people?" In all honesty, the world will do anything to stop Christians from fulfilling the glory of God. The Bible tells us that we will suffer for our faith. 1 Peter 2:21 says, "For God called you to do good, even if it means suffering, just as Christ suffered for you. He is your example, and you must follow in his steps" (NLT)(9). God called us to do good and follow in His footsteps even through adversity. If Peter tells you to live with Christ as your example, you must realize that Jesus faced some of the same sufferings we as teenagers go through. As teenagers, knowing that Jesus endured those challenges allows us to realize that we aren't alone. In fact, Jesus can relate to us; therefore, he can guide us through our obstacles.

When Jesus was faced with suffering, he spent time with God. When we face obstacles, it's our turn to follow Jesus's footsteps and utilize every difficulty as an opportunity to deepen our relationship with God. Let me give you an example of utilizing a difficult situation to deepen your relationship with God. Have you ever had a best friend betray you? I have, and we know that Jesus did, too.

In the Bible, we see that Jesus was also betrayed by one of his closest friends, His disciple Judas. Jesus's disciples were Jesus's best friends. They went everywhere and did everything together. Right before Jesus was taken to be crucified, He had a "going away" meal with His disciples. Today, we know that meal as the Last Supper. Before the Last Supper, Jesus knew that someone would betray Him. He knew that His crucifixion was just around the corner and that a betrayal would lead to the cross. Jesus even told His disciples that one of them would be the betrayer.

Do you know when someone says something, and you just get this gut-aching feeling that it's about you? Well, this was exactly the feeling Judas got because Judas immediately replied, "'Rabbi, am I the one?' And Jesus told him, 'You have said it.'" (Matthew 26:25 NLT)(9). Sure enough, we find out that Judas had already arranged to turn Jesus over to the chief priests and temple guards. The betrayal plan was that Judas was to kiss the person they were to arrest, and sure enough, Judas went up and kissed Jesus on the cheek (2).

Just like that, Jesus had been betrayed. Betrayed in a way that caused a painful and humiliating death. Now I know that your best friend's betrayal didn't end in a painful death, but my goodness, it hurts the heart. Thinking about Jesus having to die kind of makes you feel guilty for ever thinking your friend's betrayal was bad, doesn't it? The thing that stands out to me the most is that Jesus wasn't defeated. His friend's betrayal was the start of salvation for eternity. Jesus wasn't finished because He was betrayed. In fact, He used this betrayal as a part of the story of redemption.

I'm sure you can immediately think of that special person in your life who was gone way sooner than you would've liked. I know I have definitely experienced some difficult losses in my life! In Jesus' time on earth, He had a friend named Lazarus who was very, very sick. Lazarus had two sisters, Mary and Martha, who were upset (which isn't surprising knowing that their brother wasn't doing well). Mary and Martha were extremely faithful to Jesus and knew that He was the only one who could perform the impossible task of healing their brother. In faith, Mary and Martha sent word regarding Lazarus's condition to Jesus. Before Jesus arrived, Lazarus had passed. Mary and Martha met Jesus when He was on His way to town, and when he saw how upset they were "he was deeply troubled" (John 11: 33 NLT)(9). This story is where we see the shortest verse in the entire Bible: "Jesus wept" (John 11: 35 NLT)(9). Jesus, who could raise the dead and heal the sick, was upset. This verse is so important because it shows that Jesus shares in our sufferings and understands our grieving.

The next part of the story is the most important. Jesus walked to Lazarus's tomb with a crowd of people and told them to "roll the stone aside" (NLT)(9). When Jesus wanted the stone rolled aside, "Martha, the dead man's sister, protested, 'Lord, he has been dead for four days'" (NLT)(9). Jesus responded, "Didn't I tell you that you would see God's glory if you believe" (NLT)(9). What happened next is incredible. Jesus shouted for Lazarus to come out, and Lazarus walked out, ALIVE. Isn't that amazing? Now, Jesus may not raise your loved one from the dead, but He does tell us that if we have faith, God's glory will be revealed. That is why you should take every opportunity to look to Him. God is going to bring you out of the grief, hurt, and pain and use it as a testimony that will bring people to salvation.

While Jesus was on this earth, He also experienced temptation, isolation, false accusations, rejection, mockery, and beatings. Even through all the trials, He remained faithful. He obeyed the Father despite the hardships that came. Even then, Jesus never sinned. He lived a perfect life on earth, something that we as humans cannot accomplish. Yet, because of the crucifixion and the cross, our sins are forgiven, and we can trust the Holy Spirit to guide us when we are going through the same hardships. Doesn't that make you feel so comforted? Doesn't it make you feel good that the same Jesus who defeats the impossible still knows the hardships that you face every single day?

The Apostle Peter wrote to Christians to give them hope and encourage them to stay with Jesus through hard times. 1 Peter 3:13-18 says,

"Now, who will want to harm you if you are eager to do good? But even if you suffer for doing what is right, God will reward you for it. So, don't worry or be afraid of their threats. Instead, you must worship Christ as Lord of your life. And if someone asks about your hope as a believer, always be ready to explain it. But do this gently and respectfully. Keep your conscience clear. Then if people speak against you, they will be ashamed when they see what a good life you live because you belong to Christ. Remember, it is better to suffer for doing good if that is what God wants, than to suffer for doing wrong. Christ suffered for our sins once for all time. He never sinned, but he died for sinners to bring you safely home to God. He suffered physical death, but he was raised to life in the Spirit" (NLT)9.

I want to take this passage apart because it is rich in truth. In the first couple verses, Peter tells us that even if you suffer for doing good, God will reward you for it. I know that seems crazy, but hear me out. God blesses those who continue to be faithful through mockery and ridicule. God sees the kindness, love, and goodness that aren't plastered all over social media pages. However, we aren't saved by our good works, we are saved by believing in our hearts and confessing with our mouths that Jesus Christ is Lord. We do good work because of our faith, not to earn favor. Sometimes when we don't see our actions paying off, we give up. We become defeated. We let others' words, thoughts, comments, or lives distract us from trusting God. This is something that hurts my heart because we just talked about standing firm in our identity. You were made to live a life worthy of God's calling. Your identity rests in Him. Never stop living out who you are in Jesus. Continue to stand firm in Christ and trust that God will bless you for trusting Him even when faced with opposition.

In the next part of the verse, Peter tells us that God will protect us from the threats of the enemy, so we shouldn't worry. Verse 15 says, "Instead, you must worship Christ as Lord of your life" (NLT)(9). Instead of worrying, worship when we face trials, for we know that God can do so much more with our surrender than our worry. When we surrender our hearts to Him, we are free. We stop trying to do everything all by ourselves, and we allow Him control over our lives. How much easier would it be if we immediately worshipped every time we had a worry or threat that came about? Sometimes when we feel threatened, we try to defend ourselves. We try to make the situation better or make ourselves look greater. However, God wants us to worship Him and turn our self-focus to a heavenly-focus. He wants us to surrender the desire to make the situation better, and allow Him to handle it all in His mighty ways.

When we live our life for Christ, especially as adolescents, we have to be ready for questions from people. In the next part of this passage, Peter tells us to "always be ready to explain." Sometimes questions get hard. You might have someone ask you why God let something happen in their life.

YOUR IDENTITY RESTS IN HIM.

Someone might ask why you believe if you cannot see God. You may get questions about why you don't participate in the "fun" of high school. Some people might turn these questions around on you and ask why you're so picky about dating partners, or why you don't cuss.

Some of these questions might offend you at times. The questions might even make you do a double-take to make sure you heard them correctly! When you get these types of questions, it's important not to sound judgmental. The next part of the passage says, "But do this in a gentle and respectful way. Keep your conscience clear. Then if people speak against you, they will be ashamed when they see what a good life you live because you belong to Christ" (NLT)(9). At the end of the day, we want to shine God's love on people, in the hope that they will come to know Him one day. In order to do that, make sure your answers are full of love and forgiveness, even if you are hurt. Quick to listen and slow to speak is the way to approach questions. Take your answers straight from scripture and allow God to speak through you.

The final part of the passage says, "Remember, it is better to suffer for doing good if that is what God wants than to suffer for doing wrong. Christ suffered for our sins once for all time. He never sinned, but he died for sinners to bring you safely home to God. He suffered physical death, but he was raised to life in the Spirit" (NLT)(9).

Think about if you were suffering from doing wrong. On earth, there are punishments for breaking the law—speeding tickets, jail time, school suspension, etc. Our government has policies in place to discipline people when they break a law. If we think in godly terms, we sin every day. No human is perfect. I mean, give me the name of one person who hasn't told their parents they didn't eat the last cupcake on the counter when they really did. In all seriousness, though, God sent His Son, Jesus, to die on a cross so we wouldn't have to bear the weight of our sins. When you believe in your heart and confess with your mouth that Jesus Christ is Lord, you are free from your sins. You're made new in Christ. There are always consequences for our actions, but it is so much better to suffer ridicule from others for your faith than face the consequences of your sins for eternity. Fortunately, if you give your life to Jesus and trust Him each day, you reap blessings from Him.

Sometimes, the suffering we experience can feel like death. It can break us, hurt us, shatter our hearts in a million pieces, and make us question God's presence in our life. But we have hope and freedom because of the cross. Continue to live your life as a faithful, obedient, godly, respectful, loving, patient, good, self-controlled Christ-follower. People will see a difference. People will notice that God dwells within you. When the Holy Spirit is in you, there is something different about you and people recognize this.

YOU ARE FREE FROM YOUR SINS. YOU'RE MADE NEW IN CHRIST.

Trusting God when faced with suffering can be a beautiful thing. God will use your faith to glorify His goodness and love. God always wins. He will not be defeated. Therefore, turn your worry into worship, and answer people's questions with joy and gladness. Set your sights on Jesus, and utilize every difficulty as an opportunity to deepen your relationship with God.

"For God called you to do good, even if it means suffering, just as Christ suffered for you. He is your example, and you must follow in his steps."

1 Peter 2:21 (NLT)(9)

FRIENDSHIPS

If I say the word "friendship," what happens? Do inside jokes, late night conversations, laughing until your sides hurt, and dance parties flash through your head? Do you feel a sudden drop in your heart from someone who hurt you? Did your mind take you to the lie that you don't have any friends? Are you filled with joy because you have the "bestest" friend in the whole entire world?

As teenagers, we should know that finding that one true best friend is hard! Girls can be nasty! Guys can be jerks! There are so many different kinds of rules based on opinion, especially if you add relationships to the mix! I want to tell you that you can get through feeling left out, hated, lonely, unworthy, and unloved. A true, godly friendship not only refuels your soul but also your relationship with Christ. Let's first start with a situation that might just be exactly what you have experienced.

Have you ever been in a situation where you weren't allowed to be friends with your best friend's ex or talk to someone your friend doesn't like? What about the parties and get-togethers that were discussed right in front of your face, even though you weren't invited? How about the unspoken glare that one of your very best friends gave you because you received a better grade on the English test? The rules and regulations of some friendships can get so toxic if they aren't centered on Jesus. I'm sure you've already thought about a time when a similar scenario happened to you.

Despite how complicated and difficult friendships can get, good friendships are so important to find, especially in your teenage years. When you're younger, you tend to spend time around your parents and their friends' kids. As you grow into the teen stage, you transition into being around your choice of friends more than family. I'm not saying it's right; I'm saying it's reality. In order to grow in your relationship with Jesus, you have to choose the right people to guide your life on the right path.

THE RULES AND REGULATIONS OF SOME FRIENDSHIPS CAN GET SO TOXIC IF THEY AREN'T CENTERED ON JESUS.

The preteen/early teenage years are when you begin to find out who you are. You start to find out what interests you, the strengths you possess, and your purpose in this world. If you aren't surrounding yourself with people who are going to build you up, strengthen you, and cheer you on, all you will do is retreat from the opportunities to do something BIG for God. Certainly, you know that God doesn't want that for us.

God did not create us to be alone. He wants us to laugh, create memories, have fun, and have someone to share in our walk with Him. God is a God of relationships. One of the relationships he desires we have is friendship among one another. One of the earliest verses in the Bible says, "Then the Lord God said, 'It is not good for the man to be alone" (Genesis 2:18 NLT)(9). I get that everyone needs their personal space at times, but in the beginning, God created everything in the universe and declared that it was good. However, when He created Adam, he decided that Adam needed someone to accompany him. From the beginning, God created us to walk with others.

In fact, God uses everyone we come in contact with to teach us something about Him. Maybe we only know someone for a couple of months, maybe we are friends with them for the rest of our lives, but the point is that you were predestined to meet everyone who crosses your path. How that person plays a role in your life is up to God. In my life, God has used certain people to give me a new perspective, a better attitude, a more grateful heart, or even to show me that evil dwells in the world. But at the right time, God ended some of those friendships for the greater good - whether that be to increase my relationship with Him or to save me from something worse. In that case, if a friendship ends, make sure you learn something to take with you for the future. Use that interaction to grow and develop as a Christian for future encounters.

One of my favorite verses in the Bible comes from Romans 1:12. It says, "When we get together, I want to encourage you in your faith, but I also want to be encouraged by yours" (NLT)(9). This verse hit me hard the first time I read it because it is the perfect picture of what a godly friendship looks like.

There is something so special that stands in between godly friendships. The "between" part is Jesus, just in case you didn't pick up on it. You want to find someone who will walk with you on your journey with Christ. Being teenagers, life gets rough. You will mess up. Maybe you'll fail a few math tests here and there. Maybe you even say a few words that you regret. Bottom line: we're sinners. We're going to mess up; it's literally in our DNA. However, when you deliberately surround yourself with people whose foundation is in Christ, they will help you keep your eyes on Jesus through the highs and lows.

Now, I don't want you to think that because I'm a Christian, I don't have friends who aren't. I have amazing friends who I still hang out with that aren't at-church-every-Sunday, hand-raising, Christian-music,

Bible-hungry people. People think "Oh, because I'm a Christian I can't associate with people who aren't this way." No, that is not the case at all. God tells us the opposite. God tells us to make disciples within the world. To be shining lights of His glory and image. As Christians, it's our job to show non-Christians the freedom, hope, peace, love, and grace of the cross. Where people go wrong is when they start adopting non-Christian behavior. You have to be careful to know where your morals stand and how to stick to them when the people around you aren't.

The thought of opening up to a godly relationship can be difficult. You may be thinking "What is a godly friendship? What does it look like? How do I know what's a godly relationship and what's a friendship without Him? How do I get over the friendships that broke me?" Let's see what relationships without God look like, how to get over the past, and how to allow God to shift your friendships into glorifying Him.

Chapter 5

TOXIC FRIENDSHIPS

Teenagers constantly find themselves in friendships that destroy their hearts, minds, and emotional well-being. When friendships negatively interfere with a teenager's emotional well-being, they are known as toxic friendships. Because teenagers put their identity in friend groups, belonging becomes one of the most important goals of the friendship. God didn't design friendships to create stress and worry; he designed people to live and support each other in community. As teens, we need to learn that Jesus wants us to abide in Him. Through Him, you have a chance to change the dynamics of toxic friendships.

Our society has accepted toxic friendships as the norm. Teenagers have become so accustomed to being unhappy with friends, that they accept it. They think that is just how friendships work. News flash, it's not. The Bible says, "Whatever is good and perfect is a gift coming down to us from God our Father..." (James 1:17 NLT)(9). We know that God loves us and thinks of us as masterpieces. If a friendship isn't making you feel loved, how is it representing God? If you feel unhappy and miserable all the time, how is that friendship a good and perfect gift from God?

Toxic friendships may seem like a trap you will never be able to get out of. Listen, you are not alone. However, you do not deserve the constant roller coaster of emotions. God will give you the strength to leave. He will fight for you. He will be there when you feel alone. You might not even realize how toxic the situation is until you leave. If any of these bullet points describe the dynamics of your group, it's not healthy to stay.

Toxic friend groups...

- leave you out
- make you feel loved one minute and ditch you the next
- make passive-aggressive comments, putting you down
- constantly shift members

I know that might have hit a soft spot in your heart, but we're going to work through it and find victory in God's design for a friendship. Have you ever been in a situation where your friends have a party and you go have an amazing night? Dancing, making videos, laughing. You think, "It's finally going to be okay. I feel secure. I feel happy. I think I found my group." But let's pause. In this situation, the girls are looking for their worth in their friend groups. They are depending on *one* night to secure their self-worth. Instead of knowing their worth in Jesus and going to have fun with their peers, they are relying on the *result* of the night's activities and the *reaction* of their surrounding peers to solidify their identity.

TOXIC FRIEND GROUPS LEAVE YOU OUT

Let's go back. Let's say, you arrive at school on Monday feeling confident, and then no one talks to you. You are ignored, given death stares, and whispered about. Immediately, your brain starts running: What did I do wrong? Why are they mad? Did I say something? You try to ask, and you're told, "Quit creating drama. You're always trying to cause problems." They don't talk to you all night, but the next day, you walk into school and they act as if everything's fine. Confused, you ask a girl in the group what is going on, and you learn that since you are back in the group, she is out. It's her "turn" to be ignored, pushed around, and left out.

In every school, in almost every friend group, this situation happens. Sometimes the group is popular. Sometimes they think they are popular and act as if everyone adores them. Sometimes it's a group of girls trying to avoid the attention, and sometimes it's a group who is just mean to be mean. Now if you think I'm just making this up to prove a point, I did some research. Even the professionals have a term for these situations in a friend group. Psychologists call these girls "queen bees." If you think of a bee colony, the queen runs the show. She ensures the entire bee colony survives. Every little bee around her does exactly what she says when she says it... or bzz's it(3). Jennifer Powell-Lunder says that the queen bees of our lives "... seem kind and caring. They present as charming and often quite unassuming. These girls seem particularly well versed in keeping up appearances. Within their own group, they exude confidence and importance. They are quick to direct and redirect fellow group members. Their criticisms can be cutting; while a compliment from them is received with elation" (Understanding Why Queen Bees are Able to Hold Court. Psychology Today)4.

The reality is, all of us have come in contact with queen bees. When I was researching queen bees, I immediately thought they were calling my name. It was like "Okay MACY, I know you've been manipulated, ordered around, and hurt... but other girls have experienced those things, too." I don't ever want any girl, Christian or not, to feel the way queen bees make you feel. For me to make that happen, I have to speak up; there's no way I'm going to be quiet about this. Those queen bees want to have power over you. They want to try to control how you see yourself, how you view God's masterpiece. In turn, they will affect how you treat God's other masterpieces around you, and how you shine God's light on the world.

Some of the ways that queen bees make you feel:

○ They make you feel loved, adored, cherished, and accepted.
○ They make you feel as if they are the only people who know you.
○ They make you think that they have control over you.
○ They play with your emotions and constantly let you down.
○ They leave you out.
○ They say mean things about others to you.
○ They say mean things about you to others.
○ They are jealous of you.
○ They take away your happiness.
○ They enjoy making you feel pain.
○ They tell your top secrets.
○ They manipulate you until you go back to them.

I need you to know that if you're feeling like this, it's not a friendship. It's a contract. You are signing up for a broken heart. You are signing up for countless hours of tears. You are signing up to feel unloved, worthless, hated, mistreated, and betrayed. You are signing up to be a victim. If you continue to stay in a friendship that hurts you, Jennifer Powell-Lunder says that the *victims* of the queen will end up just accepting that the treatment is how girl friendships are supposed to be (Understanding Why Queen Bees are Able to Hold Court. Psychology Today)(4).

Girls. This. Is. NOT. How. God. Intended. Friendships. To. Be.

If you're in a contract, you need to get out. Girls allow the queen bee to have and abuse power because they want to feel accepted. They feel as if being accepted by the queen is the only way to their happiness and well-being.

Well, I'm here to tell you the cold hard truth. That queen wants absolutely nothing more than power. She will never make you happy because she's not even happy with herself. Most of the time, when girls are so caught up in making everyone around them miserable, the truth is they are just as broken and damaged on the inside as the people they're hurting; they're just extremely good at hiding it.

See how messed up that is! It's no wonder teenagers get so stuck in broken friendships. But I promise you, there's hope. You need to get out of those friendships in order to heal. When you leave them, it can feel intimidating, but as you trust God in this situation, he will not only heal your heart from the hurt you've experienced, but He'll bring new friends into your life that will point you to Him.

I'm going to get vulnerable for a second. I was constantly feeling hurt, left out, and unworthy. When I finally got weak enough, God gave me the strength to leave some of the friendships in my life. I'm not going to lie to you, stepping away from friendships was scary. I was vulnerable. I felt lonely. I felt like no one in the entire world would accept me. I had a lot of amazing acquaintances, but when it came to real friends, I didn't feel like I had any. I felt like I was always the "after choice." I would start getting close to a person, but as soon as that person's other friend came back around, I was out of the picture. I'm not sure if that's anything you've experienced in your life, but for me, it was hard to always feel like the second choice. I'm going to tell you a secret I learned: if Jesus is not central in your life, the relationships around you will fall apart. You cannot know your worth without knowing God.

There is going to be a void in your heart until you stop trying to find your worth in others and realize that you are worth everything to God. This world lies to us. It tells us that we are worth nothing unless we have the most popular friend group, the most Instagram followers, or the highest social status. We get so sucked into trying to make ourselves something in this world, that we completely forget how unhappy our situations are making us. Knowing your worth is the first step to getting out of those toxic relationships. It was a long process for God to heal the brokenness and put the pieces back together. I know for a fact I'm not the only one out there who's gone through friendship situations. I've seen teenagers from many different schools and states struggle in finding that one, true amazing friend.

IF JESUS IS NOT CENTRAL IN YOUR LIFE, THE RELATIONSHIPS AROUND YOU WILL FALL APART.

HEALING FROM BROKEN FRIENDSHIPS

If you are like me, when you get out of those friendships, you can feel overwhelmed. Everything you know is gone. If you feel hurt, you are not alone. It's hard to move forward and build connections with other people when all you know is manipulation. You can be so used to feeling hurt, left-out, forgotten, worthless, and unloved that when it comes to friendships, all you know is that uncomfortable feeling because all of your past ones were bad.

Maybe you're like me and you close people off. You build walls so high in your heart that not even the perfect friend could knock them down. I thought that I could keep in all of my hurt. I could bury it deep and make everything fine with new friends. But the fact was, I wasn't fine. I was broken. My past haunted me. Every time someone tried to get close, I would push them away. Sometimes God would even open new doors for me, yet I was so afraid of reliving my past that I never stepped into the doorway.

Hiding what hurt you isn't helping the One who can heal you. You need to let Jesus break down those walls and heal the past. Give your burdens to Him and allow Him to free you from the chains that held you down. Psalms 55:22 says, "Give your burdens to the Lord, and he will take care of you. He will not permit the godly to slip and fall" (NLT)9. Leaving your past behind you can be tough. It can suck the life out of you because it is a constant battle. One minute you can feel so free from that toxic friendship and everything seems fine, and the next you're staring at old pictures and videos. Pictures of you smiling, laughing, being silly, and having fun. It almost makes you believe that the friendship with them was worth it. But you know what was really worth it? Leaving.

So once you make the choice to leave, you focus on Jesus so you do not slip back into the old patterns that affected you. In 1 Peter 1, we are called to live focused on Jesus. Verse 14 says, "So you must live as God's obedient children. Don't slip back into your old ways of living to satisfy your own desires. You didn't know any better" (NLT)9. The enemy will test you when you're most vulnerable. If you're looking at the pictures and you start thinking, "they really were good friends...they were the only people who loved me...I lost the only best friends I'll ever have." That is the enemy trying to break you.

When you have those thoughts, you need to fight the enemy with truth. Remind yourself of what you went through. It should make you mad. It should create anger, not about the broken friendship but about the fact that you put up with it for so long. The way you were mistreated should make you furious. Jesus did not create you to be walked on. He created you to stand firm in your faith, no matter what. Never go back to what hurt you. You didn't know better. You didn't know the queen bee was toxic to you. You didn't know that you were constantly being hurt by the people you trusted. You didn't know that friendships could be so evil. Now you know. Now you've felt the unthinkable. You went through it. It's time to move forward, trusting God.

Remember the list of how you felt when the queen bee had power. Now let's make a list of who God says you are...

God says you are:

- Beautiful
- Loved
- Chosen
- Adopted into His family
- United
- Heard
- Identified
- Created
- His masterpiece

HE LOOKED AT YOU AND SAID, "THAT'S MY CHILD."

God knows you. He knows you better than any friend, parent, cousin, teacher, counselor, or sibling. He created you in *His* image. He chose you before you were born.

Think about it.

There are eight BILLION people in the world, and He looked at *you* and said, "that's MY child."

Let that sink in.

God knows your purpose. Jeremiah 29:11 says, "For I know the plans I have for you, says the Lord, they are plans for good and not for disaster, to give you a future and a hope" (NLT)(9).

God is showing His light through us. 2 Corinthians 5:20 says, "So we are Christ's ambassadors; God is making his appeal through us" (NLT) (9).

God hears your cry. He will *heal* you. 2 Kings 20:5 says, "I have heard your prayer and seen your tears: I will heal you" (NLT)(9).

41

God gives you strength when you are weak. Psalm 23:3 says, "He renews my strength. He guides me along right paths, bringing honor to his name" (NLT)(9).

We live in a broken world full of temptation, idols, and sin. In that broken world, hurt, sadness, and unworthy feelings occur. However, you were not chosen to be hurt. You were not chosen to suffer. You were not chosen to be manipulated. You were chosen for good. God created you for more than this world. You are called to live your life glorifying and bringing honor to God. He sent Jesus to live a perfect life, die the death that you and I deserve, and then defeated death. He is in Heaven where those who trust Him will join Him forever. That's love.

God did that for you.
To save you. To heal you. To help you. To forgive you.

When you know this truth, and you know the love that God has for you, it's impossible to look at yourself any other way. When you get out of that broken friendship, you have to know your self-worth. You were worth the ultimate sacrifice to Jesus. The only way to break down the walls from these friendships and move forward is to let Jesus in. Let Jesus into the hurt. Let Jesus into the past. Let Jesus see the parts of your heart that you kept hidden, even from yourself. Do not let a queen bee steal the promises God made about you. When you know your worth in Christ, it's time to give everything to God and move forward, holding tightly to Him.

You can tell yourself that you "trust in God" all you want, but until you fully open your heart, ask for a cleanse, and let God put the pieces back together, nothing in your life will change because you're still wrapped up in the past. Let God work in you. It's going to be uncomfortable at times. He will take you out of your comfort zone. He will place you in a new situation for His glory. However, I promise you if you let God into your heart; if you let Him mend the pieces; if you seek after Him (reading your Bible, praying, worshipping, etc.); if you refuse to give in to the people that hurt you, He will put godly people, opportunities, and His love in place of those wounds that used to devour you.

"For I know the plans I have for you, says the Lord, they are plans for good and not for disaster, to give you a future and a hope."

Jeremiah 29:11 (NLT)(9)

GODLY FRIENDSHIPS

In the last three chapters, we have talked about friendships, toxic friendships, and healing what has wounded you. It can be difficult to find other teenagers who seek godly friendship when they do not have the same faith foundation as you do. So, now it is time to talk about godly friendships and how to navigate the world of a true friendship centered on our heavenly Father. Now you might be asking, "What does that look like? How do I find godly friendships?"

When your social life is centered around people in toxic relationships, you may not know what a godly friendship looks like. To learn, let's start by taking the two words apart. According to Dictionary.com(5), the definition of friendship is "a person attached to another by feelings of affection or personal regard." Bible Study Tools(6) says, "A godly person is committed to obeying God in the world." So if we put those two definitions together, a *godly friendship* = a person attached to another by the commitment to live their lives in such a way that represents and reflects God.

Some people say the whole point of being a teenager is to "have regrets." Some teens want to party, drink, do stupid things, sneak out, and live knowing they will regret yesterday. These types of actions can bring adults to look down upon all of us.

On my 13th birthday, I was so excited. I was ready to be a teenager. I was ready for the adventures to come. But my parents continually heard comments like, "Oh boy, you have a teenager now" ... "Enjoy them liking you while you can" ... "If I hug you, is it the last hug I'll ever get" ... "Oh, teenagers are bad news." That bothered me. Growing up, I always made it my goal to follow Jesus. I remember telling my mom, "I don't want to end up changing into someone my eight year-old self wouldn't be proud of." To me, the future was a legitimate concern. I didn't know what high school would bring. I didn't know if I would step away from my faith, and I feared drifting from my values. I can confidently say that as a teenager, I have remained committed to Christ and have grown tremendously in my faith since age eight. But I grew in my faith because I looked to Jesus, one day at a time, and I'm continuing to surround myself with godliness instead of negative influences.

Being a Christian, I don't want to surround myself with trouble. I don't want to party knowing I could get in trouble, even if I didn't pick up a drink. That's a risk that could cost me the future I plan on having. That's why it is so important to have godly influences around your life. You can keep your innocence when you don't have negative peer pressure surrounding your every decision.

Proverbs 13:20 says, "Walk with the wise and become wise; associate with fools and get in trouble" (NLT)(9). When you spend time in the word of God, wisdom fills your mind because you are being enriched with truth. Finding someone who is wise to befriend takes away the fear of negative peer pressure.

One of the best things to do when trying to find godly peers is to stop and evaluate yourself. 1 Corinthians 13:4-7 says, "Love is patient and kind. Love is not jealous or boastful or proud or rude. It does not demand its way. It is not irritable, and it keeps no record of being wronged. It does not rejoice about injustice but rejoices whenever the truth wins out. Love never gives up, never loses faith, is always hopeful, and endures through every circumstance" (NLT)(9). Put your name in place of "love." Are you patient? Kind? Humble? Jealous? Boastful? Hopeful? Do a heart check.

It's so easy to expect perfection out of others without understanding your flaws. Look in the mirror. Ask God to change the imperfections. Humble yourself before Him. Let Him wash you of your impurities so that you can emulate Him in your future friendships.

Now, with that said, put your friend's name in place of "love." A true friend will have all of the qualities found in 1 Corinthians 13. No one is perfect, but when you have a Christian who is following Christ, you will see Christ shine through them. Of course, they will mess up. Of course, they will make mistakes. We're human, that's what we do. However, because of what Jesus did on the cross, those who have placed their trust in Jesus are forgiven.

So we do a heart check, we allow God to work in our hearts, now what? I think now is a great time to begin being vulnerable. Being vulnerable is tough. It can be scary. It can seem like we are giving up a part of ourselves that we kept a secret for so long. Although it can seem like a Goliath in front of you, it is necessary if you desire God-centered friendships.

Centering your friendships on God looks like this: Open up. Share your story with a godly person. Go to church with each other. Worship together. Complete a Bible study together. Pray with each other. Have conversations regarding God's work in your life. Share your faith. Be there for each other when difficulties arise. If you want a Christian friendship, you need to be ready to forgive each other through the mistakes you make.

Personally, I have seen God transform my life through my vulnerability. Relating to the broken friendships that used to overtake me, I learned that when you're faithful to Him, He'll put godly people in your life in unexpected ways.

At the perfect time, God sent me a perfect image of Himself through another girl. Because of her, I have someone to help me stay on the right path when life falls apart. That's the truth of the matter. Life will still get tough. Things will still break. However, having a Christ-centered friendship allows all of us to keep Jesus's truth during difficult times. I've grown up with this girl. We attended church together my entire childhood. She was a year older than me, but because I am old for my grade, it never seemed to hinder our friendship. We have always had the same love for Jesus, the same passion for sports, and the same love for our family and friends. We've always had a way of knowing what each other is thinking.

Best of all, we've always had a healthy relationship centered on Jesus. We've always been on the same soccer team. She was a fifth-grader, and I was a fourth-grader when I began to play for a soccer club. She was always my go-to when things in life got hard because even when we were young, we would meet up and just talk for hours. This is how I knew God truly gave me someone special.

Going into my freshman year of high school, I was so nervous about school. I was nervous that high school was going to change the person I've always been. However, this girl was my role model. She didn't conform to the world we live in. She always stood firm in her faith and stood up for what she believes in. She gave me numerous pep talks going into high school. She assured me that she wouldn't leave me, and I remember praying together. God continued to show me that this girl was supposed to be my best friend because, on a whim, we decided to be divers. One day at soccer practice, she came up and said, "Macy, we should dive this winter." I was already contemplating it because the dive coach had been trying to persuade me for years. I replied, "Well if you do it, I'll do it." So long story short, we were first-year divers in our freshman/sophomore year of high school. All of those practices and challenging mental days brought us closer.

When I think of what a true, godly friendship is, I think of her. There has never been an ounce of toxicity in our friendship, which is completely God-breathed. She is my go-to for overthinking, stressing, and ranting. She continues to prove faithful and keeps me on track in my walk with Jesus. In return, I am her sounding board, encouragement, and advocate when things get too much for her to bear. The effect that this girl has had on my life is extraordinary. She taught me how to have a godly friendship. It's because of her that I have grown so much in my relationship with Jesus.

What an amazing testimony to the life of Christian influences, right?! It is because of her that I am so passionate about all people having that godly influence in their lives. So now it's your turn. I challenge you to think about who in your life are godly examples.

- Who's the person in your life who will keep you on the right path when things get tough?
- Who has fun with you but also knows when you're hurting?
- Who can you trust to be there for you at all times?
- Who can be honest with you when you need correction?

I want you to find your friendship testimony. This can only start through vulnerability. You must allow God to work through you and your friendships. When you trust in God, you will see firsthand the love, grace, peace, joy, and forgiveness He has for you. When your eyes are opened to that, you'll start bearing fruit and treating others like God treats you.

Sometimes God will isolate you to work on your heart before He brings others along. You have to realize that you have flaws and learn from your mistakes. Philippians 2:24 says, "Then make me truly happy by agreeing wholeheartedly with each other, loving one another, and working together with one mind and purpose. Don't be selfish; don't try to impress others. Be humble, thinking of others as better than yourselves. Don't look out only for your interests, but take an interest in others, too" (NLT)(9). If you want a God-fearing friendship, you have to be a God-fearing person.The truth is, everyone needs help and guidance on the friendship path. God will show you the things you need to fix in your heart so that you are prepared to adapt the characteristics to sustain a good friendship.

GOD WILL OPEN YOUR EYES TO THE CHANGES NEEDED IN YOUR HEART.

I know in my life, God showed me that I needed to stop seeking affirmation from others and know God has abundant love for me. God showed me that I had to humble myself to be His servant. I had to stop boasting and start living in a way that was worthy of Him. God showed me that I needed to pay attention to the interests of the people around me.

God will open your eyes to the changes needed in *your* heart to be a more godly friend. However, you must be obedient to letting people come and go. Never settle for people who think poorly of you. I want you to know your worth. Everyone needs someone to walk with them on their journey to heaven, but it has to be someone who is encouraging you and not tearing you down.

I'm not saying to ditch every friendship that isn't centered on Jesus. That's the opposite of what God wants us to do. He wants us to be a light for the people who don't know Jesus. But just like you aren't supposed to "missionary date," don't try to be friends with someone just to bring them to Christ. We are leaders by the way we live, not by forcing people into our faith or passing judgment on them because they aren't the Christians we think they should be. If they see God's work in our life, the seed will be planted for God to grow their faith in Him.

Find your Jesus crew. Research shows that girls who have healthy friendships develop healthier relationships. According to Northwestern Medicine's "(5) Benefits of Healthy Relationships (7)," "being in a loving relationship, no matter what kind, can give a person a sense of well-being and purpose. In fact, it's possible that having a sense of purpose can actually add years to your life." If being in a loving friendship can add years to one's life and give them a feeling of purpose, imagine what a godly friendship can do, knowing that you are growing in a relationship with your Father in heaven.

Love is patient and kind.
Love is not jealous or
boastful or proud or rude."

1 Corinthians 13: 4-5a (NLT)(9)

RESPONSIBILITIES OF A GOOD FRIEND

The Bible is very clear about godly friendships. Finding that godly friend is one of the most amazing blessings that God will ever give you. Proverbs 27:17 says, "As iron sharpens iron, so a friend sharpens a friend" (NLT)(9). Godly friends need to sharpen each other. They need to hold each other accountable when one strays away. Sometimes, as Christians, it's easy to just think that nothing bad will happen. "If we are godly friends, we won't fight or disagree. Life won't tear us apart. We are putting God in the center, so what could go wrong? Right?" Wrong! It's the opposite! How do you build and keep that friendship when things get tough? As a Christian, it is your responsibility to help keep your friends accountable, honest, and truthful.

The enemy will try to take you away from the amazing friendship God has created. He will make disagreements seem like blow-ups, silence seem like neglect, and outside acquaintances seem like betrayal. Think about it: how many of you have gotten into an intense disagreement with your best friend and then, in a few minutes of not texting, realized that it was such a stupid thing to fight about? Even worse, how many of you have felt so guilty because you took it out of context without even realizing it?

We can fight the enemy by the way we react. God wants us to clothe ourselves in tenderhearted mercy, kindness, forgiveness, love, and patience (Colossians 3:12 NLT)(9). In a friendship, we need that. We need to react to situations with the truth. Find it in your heart to not be jealous of other people surrounding your friends. Show mercy when your friend isn't answering you right away. Don't jump to conclusions about a text message or media post. Friends need to be patient with one another.

God also gave you a responsibility to help keep your friends on the right track when they start to struggle. To keep their eyes on Jesus when they have their heads down. To help them reach for their goals when they only see two steps in front of them. To never let them settle for that relationship that will ruin them. You have a responsibility to make sure they aren't slipping away from Him.

I've seen it happen in my life. I got so scared of history repeating itself that I pushed myself away without even realizing it. A sweet girl and I met through soccer. I honestly think we were separated at birth because of how alike we are. We even have the same birthdays! She went through an extremely rough patch with queen bees and came out stronger than ever. Her path met mine, and I knew God put us together for a reason. We needed each other. She and I talked every day, and then suddenly it was every couple of days.

One day she finally texted me calling me out for being dumb and pushing myself away because I was scared she was going to leave. Thank you, Jesus! Because of her honesty and confrontation, it led us to open up and not let the enemy take over our amazing friendship that God put together. That's exactly what I'm talking about. Keep each other accountable. Instead of getting upset and pushing away, talk to one another. Tell each other what is on your heart and be honest. Do not hide the way you feel; tell someone else about it. Hiding won't fix the situation, but will just make it worse. Step up and take the initiative to refuse Satan's attempt to hurt you.

You may ask me, "Macy, if I do that, if I am honest and keep them accountable even when they don't want to hear it, will they hate me?" Well guys, here's the cold hard truth: what they need to hear and what they want to hear can be two very different things. Your friend may want to start seeing a horrible jerk of a guy and when they ask for your approval, you hesitate and say you don't think it's a good idea. It may not go over very well. Unfortunately, that is just part of the role you have to play.

Friends are going to have disagreements. Just because you don't agree on everything doesn't mean the entire friendship is over. It might stop you from speaking for a quick second, but if that person is meant to be in your life, God will always make their path cross yours again.

GOOD FRIENDS WON'T JUDGE YOU OR HATE YOU FOR SOMETHING THAT IS GOING WRONG IN YOUR LIFE

Going back to the new boyfriend example, if you know you were right, and they eventually conclude that you were right, make sure you show your friend God's grace. God knows we will disobey what He specifically tells us not to do. And yet, He still forgives us when we come to our senses and ask for forgiveness. And since we share in the glory of God because we are Christians, we are to act like Jesus and show grace despite their mistakes. You never know how God is using that experience to prepare and equip them for something in their life.

Another good thing to remember when troubles come your way: don't keep your emotions and concerns hidden. Talking it out with your friend will relieve you from the burden of keeping it hidden. They will help you. They will pray for you. They will love you. Good friends won't judge you or hate you for something that is going wrong in your life. If you keep it buried, you might end up tearing the friendship apart because you are too afraid of the confrontation.

How many of you have that one best friend who you absolutely adore, yet because you have trust issues from your past, you get extremely jealous when you see them with other friends? They might not even be hanging out, but because you see someone else's face on their private social media story, you begin to let worries slip into your mind:

- o What happened to being my best friend?
- o Did I do something that made them not want to talk to me?
- o Am I not good enough for them?

All of those negative thoughts that sneak into your mind are the enemy's way of trying to break the godly friendship that you have. It hurts. It scares you. You don't want to be hurt again, so you slowly step away from your very best friend. I know firsthand how friendships can go. Some are long-lasting, while others might only last a few weeks. I have experienced both and from what I have experienced, I believe that centering a friendship on God will withstand anything that the world may throw at you. Being a good friend does have responsibilities. It isn't easy at times. If we're being honest, it might be really hard. But when we make sure to keep our responsibilities in check, we are not only setting up a good, godly foundation, but we are also helping ourselves be a good friend in return.

DATING RELATIONSHIPS

Dating becomes a huge part of growing up. As teens get older, finding a boyfriend or girlfriend becomes one of the main focuses everyone has. Social media influences that need for a relationship with cuddling pictures, date ideas, memes, and relationship videos and posts. These posts of cute couples have misled so many teenagers into thinking that the only way to be truly satisfied is by finding a boyfriend or girlfriend.

God tells His children to find someone who reflects Him. As a teenager, it can be hard to find a person who will guide you on God's path in a dating relationship. Think about how rare it is just to find godly friends; finding a godly girl or guy can be even harder. This becomes especially difficult when many teenagers are only focused on short-term physical connections that end as quickly as it began. As a Christian teenager, you will be set apart from your peers. You will have to be strong enough to stand up for what you believe in and be disciplined not to settle for someone who could compromise that.

Throughout my teenage years, I have witnessed many teenagers destroy their mental and physical health because they compromised their beliefs for the first person that showed them attention. Listen, God made you stronger than that. He made you beautiful and wonderful. He has a plan for your life. He made every part of you with

> DO NOT COMPROMISE YOUR BELIEFS FOR THE APPROVAL OF A SIGNIFICANT OTHER!

a purpose for your good. If God made you for a specific purpose, don't waste your potential on someone who cannot see it. Listen very carefully: Do not compromise your beliefs for the approval of a significant other! I believe there are three key concepts to ensure you do not compromise your beliefs. First, know your values. Second, know your worth as an individual. Third, understand that social media relationship images are not real life and perfect all of the time.

Know Your Values

The only way to know what your values are is to actively spend time with the Lord. Luke 9:23 says, "Then he [Jesus] said to the crowd, 'If any of you wants to be my follower, you must give up your own way, take up your cross daily, and follow me" (NLT)(9). Giving up our own way is a challenge. As humans, our mindset is, "If I want something, I'm going to get it." We naturally gain motivation for reaching the goal we set for ourselves. However, in order to maintain the core values of the cross, we have to deny our worldly desires and spend time filling our minds with God's truth.

Let's say two people meet and the guy is a devoted Christian who seeks the Lord. However, the girl doesn't have interest in following Jesus. The two start talking and they develop feelings for one another. As their relationship progresses, the guy finally has a conversation about his faith with the girl. During the conversation, she mentions her negative experiences with church from her childhood and states that she has no intentions of seeking God throughout their relationship. Instead of standing up for his values, the guy dismisses her response because he likes her and doesn't want to end their relationship.

Eventually, the relationship progresses to the place where she wants to do more physically than his faith allows. He starts to question whether her proposition is truly *wrong* or not.

When you constantly obtain knowledge from God, your mindset will convert from worldly to eternal thinking. This plays a huge role in your mindset with relationships. God tells us that we should "... put to death the sinful, earthly things lurking within you. Have nothing to do with sexual immorality, impurity, lust, and evil desires" (Colossians 3:5 NLT) (9).

This verse is so important to me because it sets the tone of dating relationships. As a relationship progresses, physical boundaries may get blurred because the closeness develops between two people. This is precisely why you need to spend time in the Bible. God gives you the strength to keep your sights on Him instead of the developing desires that are created for marriage. Having someone who seeks God daily decreases the pressures that could be added from someone whose boundaries are different than yours.

Just like that, the guy dismissed his beginning faith and questioned the route in which to take moving forward. He started out seeking after what God intended for a dating relationship. He settled for someone with a different value system and found himself in a tempting situation. Now I know that not every non-Christian is going to pressure you. However, at some point down the road, there is going to be a place of conflict. In order for you to prevent that happening in your future you must know your values. Ask yourself some questions before getting into a relationship:

- o What do I want in a relationship?
- o What values and characteristics are personally important in a relationship?

- What choices and habits are deal breakers?
- What are my physical boundaries in a relationship?
- How is this person going to benefit my walk with the Lord?

In all honesty, when asking yourself these questions, are you honoring God? These questions set the tone before beginning a relationship with a guy or girl. When you know your values and you're spending time seeking God's will in a relationship, you'll begin to narrow down the people around you. Instead of settling for the first person who shows attention, be deliberate in finding someone who matches your walk with Christ.

Know your Worth

A few chapters ago, you read about standing firm in your identity. You must continue to stand firm in your identity before pursuing a dating relationship with someone else. You have to know and believe who God says you are before allowing your heart into a relationship. If you aren't confident in yourself, you'll end up placing that expectation on your significant other. I know I've seen so many relationships take a toll on the individuals because they lost who they were and placed that responsibility on the other: making the other's actions and words dictate how they felt about themselves.

I've heard of relationships that started out similar to a fairytale. When the two people began talking, there was an instant connection. They talked and talked and talked. Basically fate - if you ask either one of them. However, the longer the two were together, the more red flags had come up. For example, the girl deleted all of the other girls off of the guy's social media account. She felt threatened by the fact that the girls had contact with her boyfriend, so she removed their connection. On the other hand, the guy complained that his girlfriend didn't make enough time for him since she hung out with her friends on the weekend. The jealousy built up between the two until fights were broken out because of mistrust and personal insecurities. Before long, the two were so wrapped up in their insecurities within the relationship that they lost their worth. They based their self-worth on the actions and words of the other. Little bits and pieces of who they were chipped away because the unstable relationship had become their only adjective.

Hearing stories like that absolutely breaks my heart because God doesn't want you to live like that. God doesn't want you trapped in a situation where you are stuck. God doesn't want you so caught up in the approval of your significant other that you forget the promises He made to you. He created you fearfully and wonderfully. He knit you together down to every hair on your head. Know your worth before pursuing a dating relationship. I know that it can be hard to get out of, but if you get in a situation like the one I described, be strong enough to stand up and say, "I am worth something to God and I know my worth enough to know this isn't the way I should be treated." Maybe they will hate you. Maybe the person will stop talking to you. Maybe they will spread rumors to make you look bad, and then look like the wronged party. My attitude is, who cares? One person's inability to see your worth doesn't dictate your ability to find the godly person who will.

The last point I want you to understand before pursuing a dating relationship is:

Don't believe that every relationship you see on social media is perfect

Just typing out that point hit my heart so hard. There is so much that goes on in the background without anyone ever knowing. There are so many fights, disagreements, and toxicity that can take place. The pictures of the two people smiling, kissing, hugging, cuddling, or going on cute dates are so misleading at times. It displays a fake image of the reality of true relationships.

True relationships run out of money for expensive dates. True relationships get tired when it hits 10:00 pm because of practices, work, and/or school each day. True relationships have disagreements and arguments. Literally, ask any married couple. I have talked to so many girls and guys who have expected relationships to be easy. They expect the girl or guy to fall in their laps and always agree with everything they say. They expect their interests to be identical.

The media displays the perfect image of a relationship. Haven't you seen the Vsco text messages or picnic dates? Haven't you seen the TikTok clips of perfect little date nights? Haven't you seen posts saying "best boyfriend ever" when the entire school knows that two days ago they were about to break up?

I'm not saying that every relationship is fake. I'm just putting into perspective that people get so wrapped up in trying to find an idealized romantic relationship that they miss out on the people right in front of them. I've been guilty of it before. I've had to catch myself thinking the couples on social media are perfect and remind myself of the truth.

God knows that not every relationship will be perfect. However, there are things you can do to save yourself from compromising your values, losing your God-given value, and believing in a false idea of what a relationship should look like. God wants to help you find that godly person. As Christians, our relationship journey is going to *look* different. In order to prevent ourselves from settling, we will have single periods of our lives where we have to wait and seek God before He places a dating opportunity. Will it be hard? Yes.

Will you be disappointed when people don't turn out the way they present themselves? Yes.

Are you going to get hurt a couple of times? Absolutely.

God's preparation is allowing you to become the person in which your future spouse falls in love. It's the journey that makes the ending so bittersweet. Oh, and let me tell you, walking our journey with Jesus leading the way...well that's the journey that leads to eternity with Him.

It's natural to want to begin your search to find the godly person of your dreams. I'm going to walk you through the relationship stages to strengthen your knowledge on maintaining your faith while navigating a new stage in your life.

"... put to death the sinful, earthly things lurking within you. Have nothing to do with sexual immorality, impurity, lust, and evil desires."

Colossians 3:5 (NLT)(9)

LEARNING FROM PAST DATING RELATIONSHIPS

If you thought you had the perfect relationship, but you ended up breaking up, I'm sorry. I'm sorry you had to go through that. I've been there. You're not alone, and I'm sure you could ask any adult and they would say the same thing. Breakups are part of growing up, and almost everyone goes through at least one.

Just because breakups are normal doesn't make them any less hard. Ending a relationship - positive or negative - makes you grieve. The finality puts a rock in your stomach; it makes your eyes so puffy from tears that it hurts to see. It can make you build a wall so that no one can ever hurt you again. This is especially true if you go to the same school. Seeing a recent ex at school can leave you begging your mom to pick you up.

Breakups can leave you feeling empty, alone, hurt, forgotten, and unloved. They crush your spirit. The thoughts and memories can suck the life out of you, but don't give up, for God is with you. Don't lose faith just because one thing didn't work out. If you broke up with the wrong person, you're already one step closer to finding the one person you're supposed to be with.

There is so much you can learn from a breakup. When relationships end, they end for a reason. One person involved noticed something that wasn't working for them. Maybe it was busy schedules. Maybe it was different interests and hobbies. Maybe it was values. Maybe it was a character trait. Maybe the connection just wasn't there. Whatever it was, it was enough to warrant a breakup.

Now listen to me very carefully: don't think badly about who you are and what you offer just because one specific relationship didn't work out. You are everything someone is looking for. Everything about you: your laugh, smile, schedule, personality, appearance, jokes, family, and quirks are admirable to your future relationship partner. Not only are you admirable to your future someone, but you are perfect to God. Don't give up on God's plan to put the right person in your life. This may sound like, "Okay Macy, really?! I already know God loves me." But do you? Do you truly know that even though God sees every sin you have committed, He still views you as holy, blameless, chosen, adopted, and worthy of His love? All because of Jesus.

NOT ONLY ARE YOU ADMIRABLE TO YOUR FUTURE SOMEONE, BUT YOU ARE PERFECT TO GOD

Before I truly knew how God viewed me, I needed affirmation from people. I was too scared of what a guy might think if he knew the ugly part of me. If he knew how much I thought, analyzed, and feared. If he knew how I would make myself sick trying to get 100 things completed in one day. If he knew how perfectionism ran my life at times. Oh boy, do I wish I could go back and tell myself what I am telling you now! I used to put my happy little smile on and pretend like everything was fine - that way I didn't have to show my flaws. However, that only ended in a superficial connection because I was hiding parts of who God made me, and God didn't want me to hide.

One day during my quiet time, I turned to Ephesians. The passage changed my thought process forever. Ephesians 2:10 says, "For we are God's masterpiece. He has created us anew in Christ Jesus" (NLT)9. God called me a masterpiece. I finally realized that God created me, so knew the ugly parts about me. He knew my anxiety. He knew when I questioned Him. He knew every thought that had ever swept across my mind, and He calls me His masterpiece. When I understood that, I realized that's exactly how a partner should see me. The guy should see me through the lens that allows him to say, "She's not perfect, but she's God's masterpiece, and He's working in and through her. He created her for a purpose, and I want to walk alongside her on that journey." Unfortunately, when your girlfriend or boyfriend doesn't see you through God's lense, the relationship probably ends in a breakup. Let me tell you, just because your ex-girlfriend/boyfriend didn't see that, doesn't mean that God changed His view on you. Genuinely, God loves you more because of your flaws, and that's the kind of love that your future relationship partner should show you.

One specific thing I hate about break-ups is the aftermath. Usually, the ex-couple never talks again. They completely disappear from each other's lives. That never settled easily with me because sometimes God places amazing people in our lives for a reason; even if we misinterpreted the reasoning at first. We may think that God gave us that person for a relationship, but when the relationship doesn't work out, the amazing friendship diminishes.

Listen to me; just because dating didn't work, that doesn't mean a solid friendship couldn't continue. Have hope. God put you two together for a reason, don't make that come to a halt just because it wasn't right romantically. We are still young, remember. Instead of shutting him/her out of your life, be mature, accept the fact that it wasn't right romantically, and shift your eyes to what type of relationship God intended.

This is so relatable to someone very special in my life. He and I met in 7th grade, and I thought that God gave me the right person to start a dating relationship. (I know 7th grade, it's young, just bear with me.) We both liked each other for a while, but it just wasn't right. God had other plans.

Two years later at FCA camp, where my fire for Christ began, he and I reconnected spiritually. We gave our whole lives to Jesus, together. Since then, he and I have been best friends. Truly, best friends. We center our friendship on Jesus, and we have gotten through a whole lot of crazy together. He was there for me when I was struggling. He reminded me how much God had to offer when I couldn't see the steps in front of me. He gave me godly advice that helped me stay on God's path during hard times. He listened to my countless hours of rants, Facetime calls, tears, and anxiety break-downs. We've prayed together, talked about God's work through our lives, stepped out in faith together, biked crazy miles to take our minds' off of the world, and had some crazy adventures that I'll never forget. He is an amazing example of what a true brother in Christ should act like, and without him, I don't know where I would be today.

As teenagers, we think that every interaction with the opposite gender is an invitation for a dating relationship. We get so caught up in the idea of becoming a couple that we forget the possibility of creating a good friendship. Now, I realize no one in our day and age wants to be in the friend zone, but I wonder how many friendships people could build if the idea of dating wasn't the primary goal. My friend and I thought that a romantic relationship was the path we were supposed to go, however, when the dating idea left, we missed two years of deepening our friendship.

Now, I know that God doesn't always make you best friends with your ex. In fact, some past relationships can cut so deep that walls are built too high to accept a new, healthy, God-centered relationship. This is precisely why we have to learn from the past and allow God to heal our hearts in preparation for the future He has planned for us.

Let's say there was a couple who has been dating for over three years. They were everything to each other. The entire community cheered for them and already had the wedding planned. Holidays, birthdays, family parties, Sunday morning church services, and summers were spent together. The girl was in love, but an ongoing argument led the guy to end things. The girl was crushed. Her heart built walls and buried the hurt so deep that she forgot how to feel emotions. That lockdown resulted in the refusal to never let anyone get close. She refused to let herself feel that hurt again. She refused to let herself love anyone so much that it risked her well-being. The life she knew was gone. Over. Done. She pushed away any guy for whom she potentially could catch feelings. She would say she wanted a relationship, but because of her past, whenever a relationship presented itself, her heart went on lockdown.

Immediately, I'm sure you can think of a few names off the top of your head who have dealt with a similar story . A similar hurt. A similar relationship past where the love they once felt turned into heart-wrenching grief.

When hurt like this occurs, we have to turn to Jesus. 1 Peter 5:10 says, "After your season of suffering, God in all His grace will restore, confirm, strengthen, and establish (emphasis added) you" (NLT)(9). I remember reading that for the first time and thinking, "Wow, God really can heal me." Understand this: God will restore the hurt you once felt. He will confirm who He says you are: chosen, loved, adopted, predestined, holy, and blameless. He will strengthen your faith and give you the strength to move on into a healthier relationship. He will establish a confident hope in who He is and in the plans He has for your life.

Surrendering to Jesus in a time of hurt and struggle is the only way to heal what has been broken. Oftentimes when you have been hurt by a relationship, you accumulate an unhealthy vision of what a perfect person should be, look like, and sound like. With that image in mind, all options for a relationship are vetoed. Maybe you even have that one guy/girl who, when you follow them on Instagram, you say, "If I could only be with them." That thought immediately puts that person on a pedestal. Maybe you like him so much that when someone else comes in the picture, you shoot them down, hoping that one day the pedestal person will fall for you.

If that is you, GET. THAT. OUT. OF. YOUR. HEAD!

No one will be perfect. The only perfect person is Jesus. No person will ever live up to the standard Jesus lived out, so please don't expect them to. In fact, sometimes God will use a relationship to show you just that.

Let's say the girl crazy over the pedestal guy and that guy actually met. They began "talking" (that's where you date without an official label) and going on dates. These two were the spitting image of perfection. On paper, everything about them lined up: their faith, family dynamic, sports interest, future goals, school determination, and personality. However, when they tried a relationship, it wasn't *right*. Even the girl who had been crazy about him agreed that the relationship was missing a spark. Although they both made an effort to make it work, it always ended up feeling forced. They decided that the best thing to do was to stop forcing something that wasn't there.

See, on paper, they were perfect, and if you asked either one of them, they *should* have been the dream couple. God just had different paths cut out for the two. I love this example because it shuts down every thought that teenagers have about finding the perfect person. God is going to bless you with someone who you were created to be with, however, they are human so they won't be perfect. That was God's intent all along. God wants us to find someone who we can experience life with. He wants us to be able to pursue Him together. If we were all perfect, we wouldn't rely on God, therefore, we wouldn't need someone to help our focus stay on God's path and purpose for our lives.

God made us for relationships, but we're teenagers, remember? It's okay if it takes a couple of tries. The first guy or girl you've ever liked might not be forever. I mean, it's possible, but in reality, breakups are going to happen. And it's okay to grieve break-ups. You're allowed to be sad that someone you took an interest in wasn't right for you. However, there is so much God can teach you about yourself from a failed relationship. When you focus on what you can learn, the failed relationship will strengthen and develop you into the person someone will someday marry.

Let's look at some examples of how you can shift your thinking to further prepare you for future relationships:

- o If you broke up with someone because they want to move away to Europe, but you are the type of person who is a home-body, you learned that you need someone who will stay close to home.
- o If someone broke up with you because spending time with your family is important, and they don't have that relationship with their family, you learned that you need someone who is family-oriented.
- o If someone broke up with you because you are always busy with life, you learned that you need someone more independent.

- o If you broke up with someone because they hate your best friend, you learned that your friendship with your bestie is more important to you than that relationship.
- o If you broke up with someone because you weren't feeling that it was the right fit, you learned that sometimes even the paper-perfect person isn't meant for you.

These examples should prove that no person is a mistake. No person should be a regret. It should be a learning experience. You should learn something about yourself or what you want for your future through every dating encounter. I've seen a lot of girls and guys so blinded by their sadness that they forget to stop and realize the good it brought them. We're still teenagers, we want to have fun. We don't want more stress in our lives. Let's face it, with school and sports, we hit our max. If the dating relationship brought stress, anxiety, instability, and hurt, why are we so upset about it being over? You should be confident knowing it was fun while it lasted, but God has someone better suited for you. He has someone who is going to truly benefit you. In the meantime, you have to take a step back from reality and seek the lesson to learn from your ex-girlfriend/boyfriend. The book of Proverbs tells us that correction is good. "To learn, you must love discipline; it is stupid to hate correction" (Proverbs 12:1 NLT)(9). To learn from the past experiences, you have to discipline yourself to see what God was trying to show you through it. I know it seems hard, but when your vision is blocked by grief, anger, sadness, and confusion, you won't be able to see God's hand in the situation.

In order for you to understand the reason behind the "why" of the breakup, you have to seek God. Throughout my past dating relationships, God has made it clear to me the "why." I remember one time being so confused why my heart wasn't in it towards this great guy. He treated me right. He was fun and adventurous, but something was missing. I didn't understand why my heart felt different than my head. Honestly, I tried convincing myself I was being silly and over-analyzing the situation. However, my heart knew God was trying to tell me something.

There was one night, specifically, that I came home from a date, and I went to my room, turned on my worship music, and wrote in my journal. My journal is my escape. Writing is how I understand the thousands of thoughts in which I cannot sort. I turned in my Bible to 2 Timothy, and verse 1:19 says, "Cling to your faith in Christ, and keep your conscience clear. For some

I COULDN'T LET MY FAITH LOOSE IN A RELATIONSHIP.

people have deliberately violated their consciences; as a result, their faith has been shipwrecked" (NLT)(9). In that moment, I knew I read exactly what God wanted revealed in my heart. That's a way God speaks to us. Not by a loud voice but by the perfect passage in the right moment. When reading that message, I knew that I had to cling to my faith. I couldn't let my faith loose in a relationship. I needed to keep my conscience clear and focus on God's path. He set out a way for me to take, and I didn't want to end up shipwrecked because I lost sight of my faith. After reading that, I knew that I had to prioritize my faith in a relationship. I've always told others about the importance of a Godly dating relationship, but I had to follow that path myself. So, I stopped seeing the guy and focused on my faith. Not only did I learn that I had to prioritize my faith first, but I learned that I needed someone who also had traits that I admired. I wanted someone who was fun and adventurous. I learned so much about myself and what I wanted through seeking Jesus.

This is exactly the message I want you to hear. Maybe you were me - feeling like God was trying to tell you something but convincing yourself not to listen. Maybe you liked the qualities of your significant other but felt off about something you couldn't put a finger on. Maybe you truly have a great relationship with your significant other. To that, hats off to you! Finding a great relationship in your teenage years is rare! Whatever your position in a relationship is, I want you to remember that you're learning throughout the process.

If you recently had a break-up or have had a breakup in the past, I challenge you to take some time to seek God. I have a whole chapter called "Finding Time with Jesus" if you want to skip ahead and read right now. I challenge you in this because as teenagers, we always want to know the answers as soon as we ask the questions. I swear our impatience is in our DNA. Only by seeking Jesus will you find the lesson to the heartbreak. Maybe, in your case, God took you out of the relationships because it could've hindered the plans He had for you. Maybe God ended the relationship because He needed time with you to develop strength or trust that wasn't ready to be shared with someone else. Maybe God knew that this person wasn't the right one, and He had to stop you from being stuck with the wrong person. Maybe God knew the intentions the other had and rescued you from a situation that would have hurt you. God sees the actions that happen behind your back. God hears the conversations that you weren't a part of. God knows the intentions of people without a word ever being said. So, whatever the reason for the breakup, God did it for YOUR good, and the earlier you run to Him and begin to see that specific reason, the faster you will learn how to confront it and move on.

I want to mention that God doesn't hurt you on purpose, and He certainly doesn't cause pain in your life. The Bible tells us in James 1:17, "Whatever is good and perfect is a gift coming down to us from God our Father" (NLT)(9). If the thing you're dealing with isn't good, it's not from God. However, God helps us in our weakness (Romans 8:26), and He saves us from the things that could hurt us. So, maybe the relationship really was hurting you. However Romans 8:28 says, "God causes everything to work together for the good of those who love God and are called according to His purpose" (NLT)(9). Did you get that? God causes *everything* to work together for your good. God doesn't just make good things work out, but bad things too. He turns the bad into good. And that's exactly what you want to do with past dating relationships. Focus on the good that God created from that experience, so you can move forward with knowledge and confidence that God will bless you with a person who is going to strengthen your walk with Him.

Lord, Thank you for working all things together for my good. Thank you for showing me that you are good and true. I pray that you will open my eyes to see the good within my past experiences. Allow my heart to feel relieved knowing you hold my future with someone special. Amen.

"Whatever is good and perfect is a gift coming down to us from God our Father."

James 1:17 (NLT)(9)

WAITING FOR GOD'S TIMING

Society tries to tell teens that the only way to feel fulfilled and happy is to find someone to make them happy. If you feel a void in your heart, it's not meant to be filled with a significant other; it's God longing to fill in the missing piece. You cannot begin a relationship with another person unless you know that God is the only one who can fulfill you.

Sometimes when people want something so bad, they settle for anything that presents itself. Even worse, they're so desperate that they forget their most important relationship commitment is the one to God. Instead of waiting and soaking up what God is trying to teach them while single, they settle for the first person who shows them attention. I know this might sound harsh, but remember what I said in the chapters before: if you settle, you will always end up heartbroken. There's a good chance you'll end up wanting the relationship more than the other person, and that's not fair to anyone involved.

As Christians, it is so important to wait for God's timing. If you just got out of a relationship, don't rush into the next one. Waiting can be hard. At times, it can feel like you're waiting forever and you can grow impatient. Social media and technology have definitely not helped you out in this regard. However, good things take time. What we do during that waiting period is what is going to prepare us for God's blessing. I know this sounds crazy, but being single is an extremely important stage of your life. Even the Bible has a story where a man, Jacob, had to wait to marry the love of his life, Rachel.

When they met, it was love at first sight. They knew that they were meant for each other. They wanted to be together right away, but God had other plans. When Jacob went to get approval from Rachel's father, he was told he had to work for him for seven years to win Rachel's hand in marriage. Genesis 29:20 says, "So Jacob worked seven years to pay for Rachel. But his love for her was so strong that it seemed to him but a few days" (NLT)(9). One thing that struck me was the fact that God showed Jacob his wife, but made him work and wait until the time was right. Maybe we don't have to work with sheep and goats before pursuing a dating relationship, but if we want to find a God-centered relationship, we have to work to develop our relationship with God and wait to see His hand put the pieces in place.

I realize that waiting and being single can be annoying. It's annoying to know what you want and not be able to get it - Jacob knew he wanted to be with Rachel, but he couldn't be with her until his work was finished. Just like Jacob, every person wants a relationship. Most of us can picture our "perfect person" in our heads. Maybe the guy (or girl) you picture is a rock-star athlete with brown hair and brown eyes. Maybe the person is a fitness fanatic who loves adventures and traveling. Maybe the person you pictured is a pastor at a small-town church who breeds horses. Whatever it is, more than likely, you have painted some kind picture of the one you think you'll end up with. You might even have a checklist that you go through so that you make sure you're getting all you're looking for once you meet someone. Although that may sound amusing, it is holding you back. When you make a checklist or keep a fixed mindset on what you expect the person to be, you're building a wall. That wall will hinder you from experiencing a healthy relationship with people around you, and it will withhold you from allowing God to prepare you for the future.

God doesn't want that; He wants a relationship with you. To develop your relationship with Him, you have to actively find time with Him. Let's continue in Genesis with Jacob and Rachel. If you look back at the passage we read, notice how the verse says "... his love for her was so strong that it seemed to him but a few days." This stuck out to me. Jacob was content in the waiting because he knew the blessing that was coming.

That's what God wants us to have—contentment in the wait. While we are abiding in (working on) our relationship with Him, we will find that the fruit of the Spirit, peace, begins to reflect in and through us. In John 14:27, Jesus says, "The peace I give is a gift the world cannot give" (NLT)(9). The peace that Jesus blesses us with is how we wait faithfully. We wait in the state of contentment because we come to a place where we are so fixed on Jesus Christ that we hold firmly to the promises He gives us. If God says that He will bless us in HIS perfect timing, there's peace in the waiting because we know God is working. If God says that He is preparing us for His will, then we receive peace knowing the hurt, confusion, disappointment, and uncertainty are all building blocks to God's plan unfolding. See, we obtain peace in a troubled world because we know God holds victory in the end.

Doesn't that sound beautiful – God preparing you while you're waiting, KNOWING that your faithfulness will be blessed? Daniel 12:12 says, "Blessed are those who wait and remain until the end" (NLT)(9). God will bless you for waiting and remaining in Him. At the right time, He will reveal your forever person. I love this so much because if God is preparing you while you're waiting, He is preparing your future spouse while they're waiting as well.

Ben Stuart preached a sermon on Youtube called "Dating: Why Your Checklist Is Worthless"(8). It hit my heart because Stuart said that we should chase after the things of God during the single times in our life.

Fleeing from the youthful lust that society put in our brains, and pursuing the godly love, joy, peace, and patience instead.

AT THE RIGHT TIME, HE WILL REVEAL YOUR FOREVER PERSON.

Remember how I said that during the waiting time God wants us to abide in Him? Going further, because we abide in Jesus, we produce the fruit of the Spirit – love, joy, peace, patience, goodness, faithfulness, gentleness, and self-control. John 15:4-5 says, "Abide in me, and I in you. As the branch cannot bear fruit by itself, unless it abides in the vine, neither can you, unless you abide in me. I am the vine; you are the branches. Whoever abides in me and I in him, he it is that bears much fruit, for apart from me you can do nothing" (ESV)(10).

Think of a grapevine. The vine is established in the roots. It is firm and provides nourishment so the branches can expand and grow grapes. Our relationship with Jesus is the same way. Think of God as the roots. The roots are there to support and sustain all that is grown from it. Just like the roots, God is grounded and the anchor for our very being. He sustains our souls, heals the broken parts, and always produces good from our souls. Jesus is the vine. John 14:6 says, "Jesus told him, "I am the way, the truth, and the life. No one can come to the Father except through me" (NLT)(9). No one can go to heaven without having a relationship with Jesus. God sent Jesus to die on the cross for our sins so that those who trust Him would live in heaven with Him for eternity.

Now comes our part. We are the branches. We are connected to Jesus by a loving relationship with Him. Think of fruit being produced by a tree. When the branches have enough nutrients and water from the roots, they produce leaves and blossoms which become fruit. The fruit is the sweet part that is displayed at first glance—you know an apple tree because of the bright, vibrantly colored apples that you see. This is exactly how we are seen when we abide in Jesus. When we spend time growing and gaining "nutrients" from the Bible, we produce fruit that displays the depth of our roots.

Ben Stuart(8) also mentioned one should *chase* after Christ in singleness. When we chase after God—devoting time to Him, worshipping Him, centering our lives on Jesus, and praying for the right person—we will see people chasing Christ *alongside* us. The people that you meet on your chase are the people that God has set for you.

Like I said in the chapter before, maybe you don't meet your perfect, godly person right away. Maybe God wants to establish a foundation with Him before he reveals a romantic one with someone else. Maybe you're the person who has been pursuing a relationship with Christ for quite some time, yet you still don't see your relationship prayers being answered. Hold tightly to these verses:

- o Isaiah 60:22 says, "At the right time I, the Lord, will make it happen" (NLT)(9).
- o Ephesians 1:10, "At the right time, He will bring everything together under the authority of Christ-everything in heaven and on earth" (NLT)(9).

Notice how both of those verses begin with the phrase "At the right time..." We see these four words put together in multiple passages throughout the Bible. These four words have so much power. Remember how we were just talking about God giving us contentment in Him? We have peace and contentment because we know that God keeps His promises. We know He has something better coming for us. The words "At the right time..." shows us that we aren't waiting for just anything. Isaiah 55:9 says, "For just as the heavens are higher than the earth, so my ways are higher than your ways, and my thoughts are higher than your thoughts" (NLT)(9). It's important to note that God can see the big picture. He can see your entire life. He knows how you will meet your future spouse. He knows how to prepare you for when the time is right. Now all He needs is for you to trust in Him. He knows what your soul longs for, but He needs you to trust in the promises He has already made you.

I get it; waiting can be hard, but when God makes you wait, He may have something better in store. Hebrews 10: 35-36 says, "So do not throw away this confident trust in the Lord. Remember the great reward it brings you! Patient endurance is what you need now so that you will continue to do God's will. Then you will receive all that he has promised" (NLT)(9).

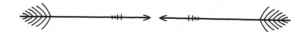

Lord, I pray for a confident trust in You and in Your mighty power. I know that You know my every need. You know what my soul longs for, and You know how to prepare me for it. Help my vision not to get cloudy. Allow me to hold firmly to the promises You made. Allow me to be faithful in the waiting periods of my life. I pray that I can abide in You and produce the fruits of the Spirit that give me peace and contentment in You. Help me to wait until Your perfect timing is revealed. Only in Your name, I pray, Amen.

GODLY DATING

In the last two chapters, we focused on learning from past dating relationships and abiding in God during the waiting stages of your life. Now I want to talk about godly relationships. You might be asking:

- o "What is a godly relationship?"
- o "How do I know if I'm in one?"
- o "What does a godly relationship look like?"
- o "How is a godly relationship different from a regular relationship?"

All of these are important foundational questions when looking to share your faith in Christ with a life partner.

I want to start at the beginning–literally. In Genesis, God created the earth, ocean, stars, sun, plants, animals, and the first man, Adam. After He made each of those things, He concluded with, "It is good." After creating Adam, God said, "It is not good for the man to be alone. I will make a helper who is just right for him" (Genesis 2:18 NLT)(9). Isn't that so interesting? God made galaxies and the depths of the oceans and was satisfied, but after making Adam, He realized that something was *missing*. The missing piece was the creation of a woman. Only a woman could qualify to be Adam's partner in the garden.

As I think about this, I'm awestruck by the fact that there's a legitimate reason why so many teens and young adults strive to feel loved in a relationship. There's a reason people who get their heart broken over and over would still rather be with that person than be alone. There's a reason people want another relationship immediately after a breakup. There's a reason people put themselves through so much for the people they love. That reason is simply the fact that God made us for relationships from the very beginning.

Now, God may have made us for relationships, but note, God wants you in a relationship that not only makes you happy but brings you closer to Him. He doesn't want you to be treated poorly, hurt (physically or emotionally), or put in a situation that could take you away from Him. That's exactly why the second part of that verse is so important to realize what a godly relationship looks like. In that specific verse, we find that God didn't just create any helper for Adam. God is way more personal than that. Instead, God said, "I will make a helper who is **just right** for him."

If God knows every thought you've ever thought. If God knows the depths of your heart. If God knows your personality, dreams, fears, struggles, sin, and mannerisms, of course, God isn't just going to match you with anyone. No, God is going to pair you with someone who fits you! He specifically knows who will strengthen your weaknesses, guide you to stand firm in the Lord when trials and tribulations come, and treat you the way you should be treated. How amazing is it to think that somewhere out there, someone was created, by God, for your good?

I love the word "helper" in this passage. The word "helper" indicates that a godly relationship is supposed to be a balanced partnership between the two involved. I've seen quite a few dating relationships in my lifetime where the relationship was more of an ownership than a partnership. Some of these ownership/controlling relationships are pretty easy to detect. Anyone heard any of these lines a few times in your life? Maybe you've even said some of them? (The words "he" and "she" are interchangeable.)

- "I need to be the number one priority in his life."
- "He's only being protective to show how much he loves me."
- "She would much rather be with her guy-friends than with me."
- "He needs to spend more time with me instead of his friends."
- "She cannot text any other guy except me."
- "He hasn't texted me for 20 minutes, but I know he was on snap 5 minutes ago."
- "A little jealousy never hurts."

Please don't take offense if you've said or heard one of these lines before. I'm not trying to target you. My point was to give you examples of common lines that lean more towards an ownership than a partnership.

I whole-heartedly believe that a godly relationship should be a partnership. If we take the word apart, we see "partner" and "ship." If a word has the suffix "ship" at the end, it means "the state of being" (Dictionary.com)11. If we combine "the state of being" with the word "partner," we get "the state of being a partner."

Now that we pulled the word apart, let's look at what specifically classifies a "partner." If we look at the synonyms of "partner," we'll find the words "associate, companion, spouse, helper" (Thesaurus.com)(12).

Hmmm, recognize any words that we've seen before? Hint: *helper*. Just to be 100% sure, let's read Genesis 2:18 again: "Then the Lord said, 'It is not good for the man to be alone. I will make a helper who is just right for him.'"(9)

Note: Being someone's helper through life isn't always going to be easy. Just like there is a responsibility to being a good friend, there is a responsibility in being a good, godly partner. When you are helping someone through their walk with Christ, it isn't ever one-sided. Remember how I said that some relationships are so toxic that it becomes an ownership? Well, this is exactly what I want to get at! People get so caught up in thoughts like, "What if he cheats on me? What if he finds a hotter girl? What if she likes someone better than me? What if I lose him?" Those thoughts take over your mind until you are worried and scared. Instead of being understanding, you might get jealous. Maybe that jealousy leads to mistrust or even a breakup.

THERE IS A RESPONSIBILITY IN BEING A GOOD, GODLY PARTNER.

Those thoughts can make you constantly worried about who your partner is with, what they are doing, and if you are going to still be with them when the night's over. That, my friend, is ownership. Not just ownership over your boyfriend or girlfriend, but those thoughts own your emotions. Unfortunately, when your emotions are played with, it can cause damage. I want you to understand what the Bible says about a godly relationship.

A true godly relationship has patience, hope, endurance, trust, love, acceptance, communication, devotion, empathy, forgiveness, and understanding. It isn't proud, envious, or rude. It doesn't rejoice about injustice (1 Corinthians 13 NLT)(9). The partnership that God brings among two people is supposed to be trustworthy. You aren't supposed to have to worry if you are allowed to be friends with other guys if you have a boyfriend. You shouldn't have to feel like you have to change who you are to make your boyfriend or girlfriend accept you. Most importantly, you cannot exceed physical boundaries to keep your boyfriend or girlfriend with you. If your relationship is draining your mental and emotional health, it isn't worth it. I can't even tell you how many people stay with the wrong person because they don't want to lose the feeling of having someone. Maybe you are being controlled so much that you don't even know what it's like to think on your own.

Listen to me:

That. Is. Not. A. Godly. Relationship.

A godly relationship should be two people helping each other through careers, emotional breakdowns, decision-making, and, of course, helping each other enjoy the beautiful moments. God doesn't want you to have to go through the hard times alone, but He certainly didn't intend for you to spend the joyous moments by yourself either. We are told this specifically in Ecclesiastes 4:9: "Two people are better than one, for they can help each other succeed" (NLT)(9). God tells us that two are better than one. So now it's time to step out in faith to find the one intended for you. If you think everything will just magically fall into place without having to move a muscle, you're wrong. You cannot sit on the couch every Saturday night and expect the man (or women) of your dreams to come prancing through the door. Wouldn't that be nice? My goodness, a girl could dream! Unfortunately, the world doesn't work like that. Therefore, we have work to do.

God calls us to step out in faith - knowing that He is guiding the way. You have to take the leap of faith to talk to the cute girl or guy in chemistry. You have to take the leap of faith to agree to go on a date with that one guy who just won't give up on you. You also might have to take the leap of faith to break up with the guy or girl who controls you and makes you feel worthless. Unfortunately, leaps of faith can go both ways. There are so many blessings that can come from obeying what God has laid on your heart - even if it seems difficult.

Remember how I said that every relationship is a chance to grow as a person? It's a chance to learn and find out what you want and need from a partner. To find a godly relationship with someone, you need to know what to look for. When dating, be sure to stand firm in your faith. Be upfront about what you believe in and start a biblical conversation. If you want to have that godly relationship where you pray together, go to church worship nights, and grow as God's children, you need to have the same foundation. God tells us that we must be equally yoked, that we cannot team up with unbelievers in a marriage (2 Corinthians 6:14 NLT)(9).

I don't want to contradict myself because God tells us that we must go and make disciples among the nations (Matthew 28: 19 NLT)(9). However, in a relationship, if you are in two different spots spiritually - it's hard to grow together. Now, if the other person is a Christian and wants to get into the Word more, that's completely different than trying to force someone to read the Bible when they are adamantly opposed.

Don't get me wrong, as a Christian, it can be hard to find someone who is equally yoked. It is not the most popular thing to do, especially for teenagers. However, I believe that God will bless you for waiting and being faithful. When dating, don't get too in-depth when the person isn't attuned to your faith. Shut it down fast; that way no one gets hurt. Your faith is a lasting foundation. Find someone who is going to match that, and don't settle for any less.

Let God bless you with the person who is going to help you through life. God will match you with the person who you connect to spiritually. Take a leap of faith and find out what God is trying to show you through every encounter. Abide in Christ and see how the fruit of the Spirit comes alive within your relationships. If you are in an ownership–get out! Be strong enough to know your worth and know that God has so much more for you. He created someone to walk alongside and support you. Allow your relationship to be a loving partnership in your journey to heaven.

"It is good." After creating Adam, God said, "It is not good for the man to be alone. I will make a helper who is just right for him."

Genesis 2:18 (NLT)(9)

FINDING TIME WITH JESUS

In a world full of schedules, it can be hard to take time out of your day to seek God. One of the most common sentences I hear is, "I just don't have time." The thing is, no one has "time" to complete every task you want to do when you want to do it. Even if you try your hardest, it'll always come down to there only being 24 hours in a day. However, you prioritize the activities that are of the utmost importance.

There was a time in my life when I had to choose. I had to choose between continuing my dance career or pursuing a more vigorous club soccer team. It can feel like the end of the world when having to decide between two choices, especially sports. In my mind, I thought I could do both. Dance practice would get out earlier, so following practice, I could go to soccer. I didn't want to have to decide. I loved gliding across the floor to the count of the song. I loved the lights, the nerves, the performances, even if I had to put on five pounds of makeup for a three-minute dance. There was something special about performing. At the same time, I grew up with grass stains and shin guards. Since I was three, I had known how to move the ball up the field and into the goal. If I quit, what would I miss out on? What would happen if I regretted the choice I made? I had to learn to prioritize what renewed my soul. I had to choose one so I could grow and focus on developing in one area instead of half-participating in two.

This picture is exactly what I want you to imagine when seeking time with the Lord. In life, you only have so many days. There are only 24 hours to work with in a day. With unlimited decisions, don't make God conform to your schedule; rather, conform your schedule to God. The older you get, the more decisions you'll have to make. One that should remain constant is deliberately making time to spend with God. When you make time for Jesus, you'll see His hand guide you in the direction He wants your life to go. Psalms 32:8 says, "The Lord says, 'I will guide you along the best pathway for your life. I will advise you and watch over you'" (NLT)(9). Spending time with God is the most important thing to prioritize in your life. It is the one thing that you should never have to compromise. It fulfills your spiritual hunger.

I know you're thinking, "Hunger? Like food?" Of course, not food. Think about it though: when you're hungry, what happens? Your stomach starts to hurt. You might get a little cranky. You might feel light-headed. Your body begins to react because it needs the energy from food. We get like that spiritually. We need God to survive. We might get a little cranky, upset, overwhelmed, or confused when we're faced with a problem. Our stomachs might ache when facing hardships. Our body might react physically to our emotional distress. However, we can't carry our burdens, worry, fear, mistakes, past, or our daily struggles alone. We can't. It is too much to bear. The weight of those burdens will sink us until we can't function. Matthew 11:28 says, "Come to me, all of you who are weary and carry heavy burdens, and I will give you rest" (NLT)(9). If this isn't crystal clear, I don't know how else to explain. God doesn't just want you to open your Bible for His sake, but to remind you of the promises He holds true. He wants you to be comforted in His peace, safety, and joy. He wants to remind you of your worth and value in Him.

I want to share a story from the gospel of John in the New Testament. Jesus and His disciples were sitting on a hill when a crowd of 5,000 people came to greet Jesus. Jesus (already knowing what to do) turned and asked His disciple, Philip, how they were going to feed everyone. Philip replied, "Even if we worked for months, we wouldn't have enough money to feed them" (John 6:7 NLT)(9). The other disciples, becoming aware of the situation, said they found a boy with two fish and five loaves of bread. Taking the fish and bread, Jesus immediately told the crowd to sit down. "Jesus took the loaves, gave thanks to God, and distributed them to the people. Afterwards he did the same with the fish. And they all ate as much as they wanted" (John 6:11 NLT)(9). When everyone's hunger was satisfied, Jesus sent the disciples to fetch the leftovers. The disciples came back with twelve baskets of bread.

I love this story because it enhances the power of God satisfying hunger. God does the exact same thing with our spiritual hunger. When we take time to abide in Him, we begin to see His hand in the impossible. When we have barely any hope left, God gives us an everlasting mindset. When we feel like we're bearing too much, God will lift the weight from our shoulders. When we feel lost, God will give us a name. There is nothing too big for the power of God. He takes what is minimal in our lives and makes it abundant.

Have you ever seen the famous present people give that has coffee beans in a glass casing with "Use in Case of Emergency" on the front label? I'm pretty sure at least one of my teachers has one hung up in their classroom every year. We don't want to do that with our relationship with God. We don't want to put our Bibles in a glass casing only to break "for emergencies." God wants to have a closer relationship with you than that. He wants you to fully depend on Him. He wants to help guide you on the best pathway for your life. However, in order to accomplish that goal, we must be disciplined enough to open our Bible daily. Joshua 1:8 says, "Study the Book of Instruction continually. Meditate on it day and night so you will be sure to obey everything written in it. Only then will you prosper and succeed in all you do" (NLT)(9). God tells us to "Study the Book of Instruction continually." Hint: that's the Bible. Notice the word "continually." For us to prosper as Christians, we have to be in the Bible more than every Sunday. Now, if you tell yourself "I have to read the Bible every day," it will only make you procrastinate. So, make it a habit, starting today.

WHEN YOU DON'T KNOW THE ANSWER, PRAY.

Starting my freshman year, I knew I wanted my life to look different. Coming back from FCA (Fellowship of Christian Athletes) camp, I knew I had to center my life around Jesus, instead of trying to fit Jesus into my life. This can seem intimidating at first. I felt overwhelmed. I thought to myself, "When am I going to do this? How do I know where to start or what to read?" Side note: When you don't know where to start, God does. When you don't know the answer, pray.

Praying is a key to your daily biblical routine. God wants to be in your life. He wants to hear from you. He wants to help you understand, not only His word, but also how to live a life in Him. Jesus tells us that when we seek God, we will find Him. Matthew 7:8 says, "For everyone who asks, receives. Everyone who seeks, finds. And to everyone who knocks, the door will be opened" (NLT)(9). In order to ask, we must pray. Prayer is a direct conversation with God. Before you open your Bible, pray that you will receive His word in your heart and understand what He is trying to say. Spend time in prayer asking what He's trying to teach you through the passage and how He's using it to strengthen and equip you. The more you pray, the more developed your relationship with God will become.

When I was questioning where to start, I took it upon myself to pray. I prayed about finding time with Jesus and how to begin my studies.

Luckily, God always answers prayers, especially when they're meant to glorify Him. I felt the Holy Spirit guide me toward reading my Bible in the morning. I decided to wake up a little earlier each morning instead of staying up later, especially because I am such a grandma when it comes to going to bed. I started waking up a half-hour earlier, so I could read the Bible before school. I read a little section and wrote down one verse that stood out to me. I made that a habit. I found that I would wake up and the passage I read was *exactly* what my heart needed to hear that morning.

One time specifically, I went to bed upset. I didn't know the words to pray. I didn't know where God was at during my struggle. I was His child, yet it felt like He didn't even know me. I was thinking, "If He knew me, why would I be in a spot of fear? Why would I feel so weak? Why would I feel useless?"

The next morning, my Bible passage was Romans 8:26-30.

"And the Holy Spirit helps us in our weakness. For example, we don't know what God wants us to pray for. But the Holy Spirit prays for us with groanings that cannot be expressed in words. And the Father who knows all hearts knows what the Spirit is saying, for the Spirit pleads for us believers in harmony with God's own will. And we know that God causes everything to work together for the good of those who love God and are called according to his purpose for them. For God knew his people in advance, and he chose them to become like his Son so that his Son would be the firstborn among many brothers and sisters. And having chosen them, he called them to come to him. And having called them, he gave them right standing with himself. And having given them right standing, he gave them his glory" (NLT)(9).

It was a God moment I will never forget. I got such a clarification that I was God's child. That God knew my prayers. That I was chosen before the world was even a thought. I was called to His purpose. He has a plan for me. He loves me. All because I opened my Bible to seek an answer.

Do you see what I'm saying? When you begin to seek Jesus, He will help you in your weaknesses. He will be present and give you wisdom and comfort in order to get out of a negative mindset. He will remind you of His purpose for your life and allow you to see the love He has for you. You will understand your worth in His holy name.

When you sit down with the Lord, start small and simple. Find a quiet place - alone from the noise of this world. I have found that isolating myself has made me more aware of God's presence and words through scripture. Maybe you could sit in your car for five minutes before going inside. Maybe you could go to a coffee shop or park to isolate yourself. If you cannot drive, maybe the best place is a small room in your house or your bedroom. It doesn't have to be anything fancy, it just has to be consistent. Consistency allows repetition to become a habit.

WHEN YOU SIT DOWN WITH THE LORD, START SMALL AND SIMPLE.

Remember how I said that I got up earlier in order to read the Bible before my day started? That was a routine I began and stuck with until it was my normal. I realize that not everyone is a morning person like I am, but that doesn't mean you cannot find time for God. If you are a night owl, make it a priority to read the Bible right before you go to bed. Maybe you aren't either of those things. That's 100% acceptable; set an alarm on your phone, so that you know when it is time to sit down with the Lord. God doesn't want you to make spending time with Him a dreadful burden. He only wants your faithful obedience.

Starting habits can be difficult. You will have setbacks. We're all humans who still struggle with sin, but God gives us unending grace and has covered our mistakes on the Cross. As a Christian, you'll have to give yourself some grace, too. You cannot condemn yourself for messing up. When toddlers begin to walk, they don't stand up and run. It takes practice. One step at a time until they get enough balance to take multiple steps in a row. When the toddlers are persistent in trying, they'll eventually start to run. When they fall, their parents aren't screaming at them. In fact, they're cheering them on for taking the first step. This is the same way with God. Let's say you miss a day of reading your Bible. God isn't going to turn His back on you, rather He'll offer His hand to help you stand back up. He's like the parent, cheering you on for taking the first step. Likewise, you shouldn't give up on seeking God because you've slipped once. Stand back up, get your balance, and take another step towards Him. When you give yourself grace and realize God's not condemning you, you'll eventually be running toward Him.

Before you begin, it's important to know that scripture is an open conversation with God. 2 Timothy 3:16-17 says, "All scripture is inspired by God and is useful to teach us what is true and to make us realize what is wrong in our lives. It corrects us when we are wrong and teaches us to do what is right. God uses it to prepare and equip his people to do every good work" (NLT)(9). This verse shows us that God uses scripture to speak to us. Let me ask you a question: When you're having a good conversation with someone, is it formal and proper? Are you using perfect English with proper manners? If not, then don't try to make your time with God that way. He doesn't want perfection in your prayers; He wants honesty and authenticity. When you pray, let God know what is on your heart, share with Him the needs you have (as well as the needs of others), and praise Him for who He is. Thank Him for the amazing things He's done and doing in your life.

Different people have different suggestions for starting your biblical study. If you're a new Christian, I recommend getting an understanding of who Jesus is by reading the Gospels (Matthew, Mark, Luke, or John). The Gospels are basically a biography of Jesus. Another place people say to start is Ephesians. Ephesians helped me understand just who I am in Christ and what He does for me. If you already have a firm understanding of who Jesus is, you could choose to begin your daily routine in Psalms. The Psalms are suggested by many pastors because of the rich songs, applications, and advice found there. The Psalms are also an incredible model for how to pray through difficult times and how those difficult times lead us to worship.

I realize that reading the Bible can seem intimidating at first. All of the words, pages, and books can seem overwhelming. Just take it one passage at a time. It's not a race to see how much you cover; it's simply the depth of what a single verse can mean. One verse can be so powerful. There's a common misconception that you have to read multiple chapters of the Bible when you sit down with God. While reading the whole Bible is great, understanding the depth of God's word should be your first goal.

I pray that these simple tips allow your spiritual hunger to be filled with the Word of God. When you get in the habit of spending time with Jesus, you will see Him move mountains in your life. You will start to live out your faith. You will see God sanctify your life to be a representation of Him. You will bear the fruit of the Spirit and understand who He created you to be. I promise if you prioritize spending time in the Word, you will see darkness turn into light.

LIVING OUT YOUR FAITH

The more you learn and spend time seeking after God, the more you will feel led to share the amazing things God has done and is doing in your life. Actually, that's exactly what God wants. He wants us to share our faith so that we can make disciples. Matthew 28: 19-20 says, "Therefore, go and make disciples of all the nations, baptizing them in the name of the Father and the Son and the Holy Spirit. Teach these new disciples to obey all the commands I have given you. And be sure of this: I am with you always, even to the end of the age" (NLT)(9).

Jesus wants us to share our faith in order to bring other people home. That can feel intimidating. I know when God was telling me to get out of my comfort zone for Him I argued, "God I just figured out my relationship with You, how am I supposed to lead others?" Although, notice the last sentence of the verse above: "I am with you always, even to the end of the age" (NLT)(10). God is with us. He has given us His Holy Spirit, who gives the tools and knowledge to shine for Him. He isn't just throwing us out into the wilderness to fend for ourselves! He is guiding us and helping us as we step out in faith for Him.

As teenagers, it can be scary accepting the invite to step out of your comfort zone for Jesus. The world focuses on our weakness to tell us that we aren't good enough, that people will make fun of us, or that we are too young to fulfill what God is calling us to do. I'm here to tell you that this is a lie. 1 Timothy 4:12 says, "Don't let anyone think less of you because you are young. Be an example to all believers in what you say, in the way you live, in your love, your faith, and your purity" (NLT)(9).

Just because we are young does not mean that we are incapable of standing tall for Jesus. Think about David and Goliath. Despite his size, David stood up to Goliath in God's honor and won. Don't ever let anyone tell you that you are too young to do something, especially if God is knocking on your heart. If God is calling you to do something, He's not going to stop until it is complete.

There was a time in my life where I felt like God was calling me to create a social media platform for sharing scripture. I didn't know what He wanted me to do specifically, but I knew that He was preparing something special. I felt led to begin sharing and using my writing talents to reach other people. I began to pray and focus on my relationship with Christ. The more I got into the Word, the more I longed for my peers to know the goodness of God.

2 Timothy 3:16-17 says, "All scripture is inspired by God and is useful to teach us what is true and to make us realize what is wrong in our lives. It corrects us when we are wrong and teaches us to do what is right. God uses it to prepare and equip His people to do every good work" (NLT)(9). I found that the scripture I was reading just made my heart light up! Each and every time I read it, I felt empowered to live in the way I was experiencing during my quiet time.

After lots of prayer and time with Jesus, I decided to make an Instagram account, specifically to share Jesus with my community during that time. When I started the page, I thought it was going to be simple - just sharing the passages that God led me to in the mornings, plus I wrote my interpretation in the caption. I soon found out that people liked the encouragement! This all took place right as the coronavirus was introduced into our lives. I felt led to step out even more and make a video reminding people that God was with them during the rough time. I didn't want to create a fuss, but I needed a place to share it, so I posted it on YouTube and shared it via Facebook. I trusted that God was going to use it to inspire the people He needed it to. While it didn't go viral, it reached the people that God intended, and I was so encouraged and overwhelmed with the Spirit of God that I began to make more videos.

Stepping out in your faith doesn't have to be something dramatic. It can be as simple as sharing a verse on your Instagram story, smiling at someone you pass in the hallway, or asking someone how their day was. Likewise, you could start a ministry page for sharing verses and devotionals. Whatever it is, God will use it to work in the lives of those around you.

I REFUSE TO BELIEVE THAT WE ARE TOO YOUNG TO HAVE AN IMPACT.

I refuse to believe that we are too young to have an impact. If you abide in God and allow Him to use you, you will see your life explode for His glory. Matthew 17:20 says, "I tell you the truth if you had faith even as small as a mustard seed, you could say to this mountain, 'Move from here to there,' and it would move. Nothing would be impossible" (NLT)(9). Jesus told His disciples that faith the size of a mustard seed was enough to move an entire mountain. God will use you. It's up to you to let Him. Let Him use the faith in your heart to move mountains in other people's lives.

Sometimes this faith can be scary. Fear and doubt overtake your thinking, and you feel like you are not good enough. I know there were months during the writing of this book that I stopped completely because I let doubt cloud my vision. I was so blinded by the thought of what my peers and community would think if a teenager wrote a book. Therefore, I stopped doing God's will. I stopped having faith that God would take care of me and use my fingers to type each and every word. I forgot Who I was doing it for. Although, as I said, if God wants to do something through you, He's not going to give up on you. Every single time I would watch a sermon or read about completing God's will, this book came to mind.

Looking back, I want to tell you to never be afraid of what others might say about living out God's will. Psalm 18:2 says, "The Lord is my rock, my fortress, and my savior; my God is my rock, in whom I find protection. He is my shield, the power that saves me, and my place of safety" (NLT)(9). The Lord is your shield. He is going to protect you from the negative words of nonbelievers. I'm not saying that God is going to keep you from unkind words. Unfortunately, that's not possible in the world we live in. However, God is going to strengthen you and be your place of safety to run. He is going to provide you with the words to say, knowledge to grow, answers to questions, and the authority of His truth. He isn't going to leave you when things get tough, rather, He is going to uphold you to continue shining brightly for Him.

Yes, other people will have opinions. Other people might say things about your posts or ignore you when you're talking about Jesus. However, never let that stop you from continuing to live out your faith. If I let people's opinions stop me, you wouldn't be reading this book right now. In order to not let opinions stop you, you have to get to a place where you have peace in knowing what God called you to do; that's the only thing you can rest in. Use that peace to show other people how good God is. Show them the amazing love and grace that He continues to give us. Give them a little taste of our Holy Father.

You may be asking, "Macy, my life is busy enough! How am I supposed to have time to live out what God is calling me to do?"

If you want to talk about busy, *my* life is busy. I am a two-sport athlete who consistently competes in both sports year-round. I dive during the high school soccer season, and I go to club soccer practices during dive season. It's a non-stop after school commitment. Along with sports, I'm class president, an FCA (Fellowship of Christian Athletes) huddle leader, involved in GCF (Girls Christian Fellowship), a part of the Superintendent Advisory Council, and A Capella Choir. I also sing with the worship band on Sunday mornings and run a homemade cupcake business called Cupcake Perfect. I'm not trying to one-up you. I'm getting to the point, I promise. When I felt led to step out and write this book, I was in the middle of total quarantine in March of 2020. I was at a complete halt in my busy schedule. I was so used to a busy life that when it stopped, I had no idea what to do with myself. God used that time to allow me to begin this book.

After lockdown, when life got busy again, I stopped my book altogether. My excuse was, "I'm too busy," but as I said, I actually let doubt and fear cloud my vision. God gave me a chance to pick this book back up during a quarantine I was placed into in July 2020. I'm pretty sure I read one chapter

IT WAS LIKE AN ATTACHMENT GOD HAD STUCK ON MY HEART.

and thought, "This is stupid," and didn't look at it again. God didn't let that settle. I already mentioned that every time I would hear a sermon or read about God's calling, my mind immediately came back to this book. I couldn't let it go. It was like an attachment God had stuck to my heart.

In October 2020, I was given yet another chance to finish it when I was exposed to COVID-19 and put into a second quarantine. I admit I went through a couple of chapters that time, but I was too consumed with school. At least, that's what I told myself. I was so focused on how upset I was regarding my circumstances that I didn't even view the extra time as the blessing that it could have been.

Once I was finally back in the real world, there was one Sunday morning where it all hit me. It was like God was speaking to me straight through the pastor's mouth. I was Jonah. I was running. I was running from the one thing God called me to do. Not only was I running, but I was making excuses and doubting if God had the power to provide for me. I was doubting if I was worthy enough to write a whole book. If I was smart enough. If I would even say the right words. It was then that I realized quarantine was my whale. God sent a whale to swallow Jonah for three days in order to sit him down and talk. Likewise, God had sat me down in two quarantines, so far.

After that service, I cried. I was honestly upset with myself for knowing exactly what I *should* be doing and not doing it. For hearing God speak to me and not listening. For not taking advantage of the time God gave me to finish my book.

This shouldn't surprise you at this point, but shortly after that sermon I was placed in a third quarantine from another exposure at school. Now, I promise you, I wasn't trying to get quarantined. I didn't enjoy sitting out of my commitments and not seeing my friends. But God had other plans. This was my third quarantine.

As I was sitting in the office waiting to be sent home, I broke down. It became so very clear that God deliberately gave me this time to complete what I needed to complete–this book. It was like God finally said, "All right, Macy, you're done running." Unfathomable peace swept across me as I raced home, ran upstairs, and began typing.

That's my story. I know that you may be even busier than I was. Maybe you feel like God is not leading you to do anything. I encourage you to get attuned to Him. Spend time in the Word and go from there. In His perfect timing, He will assign the perfect opportunity. I am so excited to see how God uses you!

When sharing the Word, don't shove it down non-believers' throats. Meaning: never try to *force* religion on someone. As Christians, it's our job to plant the seed of faith and let God do the growing. 1 Corinthians 3:6-7 says, "I planted the seed in your heart, and Apollos watered it, but it was God who made it grow. It's not important who does the planting, or who does the watering. What's important is that God makes the seed grow" (NLT)(9). Planting the seed in someone's heart is simply telling them about Jesus Christ. Watering the seed would be as simple as always showing them the godly way to live. Remember: actions speak louder than words! If you live your life as an example of who He is, they will know something's different. Your actions could water the seed of faith. God is the one who makes the seed grow. He's the one who can take the seed and transform peoples' hearts.

With that being said, let your faith shine to the world. Don't hide the light God placed in your heart. Abide in Jesus and let the fruits of the spirit - love, joy, peace, patience, kindness, goodness, faithfulness, and self control - rule in your heart. Let the Root produce the fruit so that people know who you are in Jesus. Don't be overbearing, but let God use you to reach other people. Do not think you are too young, and never allow doubt to hinder the work God is doing through you. God will give you the time to complete what He is calling you to do. He will empower and shield you. He will equip you with scripture to encourage you. Don't give up when the world fills you with uncertainty, but trust in God to continue to live out the fire He placed inside.

"The Lord is my rock, my fortress, and my savior; my God is my rock, in whom I find protection. He is my shield, the power that saves me, and my place of safety."

Psalm 18:2 (NLT)(9)

My Testimony

My testimony starts like many other born-and-raised Christians. I grew up in a Christian home with Christian parents. I went to a Catholic school for three years and church most Sundays and Wednesdays. I've had a love for Jesus since I was three years old and have always been a well-behaved kid. I was (and still am) a perfectionist; we will get back to that. However, despite my positive upbringing, I have struggled with anxiety my entire life. I was super good at always worrying about someone, something, and EVERYTHING!

I would have described myself as a strong Christian, constantly hungry for God's Word. Although my faith was strong, my fear was stronger. I allowed anxieties to run my life pretty severely throughout middle school in areas including sports, grades, friendships, self-confidence, self-worth, and others' opinions. I was just trying to be as perfect as I could be. I thought if I was perfect enough, people would stop saying mean things about me. The more the chatter came, the more I withdrew from my faith. I thought that the only way people would accept me was if I "calmed down" my Christian lifestyle.

Now, I realize everyone has some fears, but mine were different. You see, my fears kept me from ever going outside my comfort zone. I refused to go to camps, other people's houses, school, or places where

I wouldn't know anyone. I used my sports to escape the fears of everything else. My anxiety was compounded with medical struggles, too. From fourth grade to eighth grade, doctors spent countless hours trying to decide what was anxiety and what was wrong with my body. Everything I ate made me sick, so I was afraid to eat anything besides a few basic "safe foods." The worst part was, since I didn't know my diagnosis, I never told anyone about my pain and worry. My medical issues got so difficult that, in eighth grade, I missed over thirty days of school.

In eighth grade, I ended up with stress fractures in my back from overuse. This injury completely took me away from soccer, the only thing that helped me escape my life. Not only was I struggling with not playing, but my stomach pains increased, so I stopped eating full meals. I feared food would make me sicker. Since I stopped taking care of my health, I was absolutely broken–spiritually and physically. I knew something had to change, but I had no motivation. I never allowed God to give me strength because, to be honest, I thought I could handle it on my own.

In the summer of 2019, I decided I wasn't going to play basketball anymore (something I did well) because of the stress it caused me. It was an extremely tough decision that truly took the life out of me. Along with giving up basketball, my friends were super inconsistent at that time. I was confused about where I stood in my friend group. As if that weren't enough, I had just ended my relationship with my first boyfriend. By that point, nothing in my life was constant, and I constantly felt defeated.

That summer I went on an amazing vacation. This trip was 4,000 miles from home and allowed me to experience new perspectives and cultures. I discovered beautiful gardens and mountains in Germany, gorgeous cities in Italy, and amazing restaurants in Switzerland. Since the time change was so different, the only time I could talk to my friends was at 3:00 am. It honestly gave me a break from the constant stress of keeping up with social media. Therefore, I was able to take a break from the stress at home and enjoy my first week of vacation.

After the first week went by and I returned to my phone, I felt a huge void in my heart from all of the things that were happening without me. I was supposed to be living my best life on vacation, and what I was doing was trying to avoid my struggles. A huge epiphany hit me that I wasn't happy. If I was home, I wanted to be somewhere else. If I was somewhere else, I wanted to be home. No matter what I did, there was always a void in my heart.

That build-up led to an extreme breakdown on June 24th, 2019. I was up late talking to my friend about my recent breakup. I was so upset. I don't know why I was upset, but everything that had been accumulating hit me hard. I tried to take my mind off of my emotions, so I looked at my pictures. I save inspirational quotes, so I wanted to see if anything could make me feel happier, relieved, or hopeful. I saw a quote that I saved from days prior, saying, "The thing you're waiting and praying for may be closer than you think."

Immediately I prayed that God would take away my void. I prayed that I would know how much I meant to Him. That He would heal me from all the hurt I experienced. When I said "amen," I felt confidence build as I solidified and identified the person who I was in Christ. I felt my entire body glow with the Holy Spirit. It was at that moment that I got on my phone and wrote, "I am a beautiful, fit, compassionate, loving, caring, ambitious, smart, family-oriented, friendly, special girl who is 100% God's Child." No matter how many words slip out of my mouth, mistakes I make, friends I betray, and family I disappoint, God will love me. He will forgive me. By His grace I am given every single thing I have: my family, friends, sports, talents, strands of hair, eyes, house, school, and generation. God doesn't need me to be perfect, nor does He want me to be. God wants me to be a light for Him. It doesn't matter how many times I mess up. My purpose remains because of Jesus's grace on the cross. I am done having stress bring me so far down that I can't even see the next step I take. Not every day is going to be sunshine and rainbows, and not a day went by that the devil didn't torment Jesus, yet Jesus stuck with God through the storm. God doesn't give us what we can handle. God helps us handle what we are given. I don't have to try to be perfect anymore. I can look toward the perfect God to help me get through it all.

Later that summer, I went to FCA (Fellowship of Christian Athletes) camp. On Tuesday, July 16th, we had the last chapel of the night, and it changed my life forever. Barb Roose, the speaker, was talking to us about "going beyond" in our faith. Going beyond meant going more deeply with our faith to make sure that we were living every single day in Jesus and not just with Jesus. When she was wrapping up, the song "Bigger Than I Thought" by Passion(1) began. The song specifically states,

"So I throw all my cares before you, my doubts and fears don't scare you. You're bigger than I thought you were."

At that moment, I broke down in uncontrollable tears. I felt God fully take hold of my heart. I've never felt so wrapped in love. I felt God's presence take everything I've ever struggled with and break the chains that once held me. I remember describing it as "my heart was glowing." Following that chapel, my friends and I all sat down and confessed what we had gone through. We expressed what was on our hearts and what broke us. I sat there and listened to the Holy Spirit work. I finally let out everything I had kept in for so long, and I surrendered everything to Jesus.

After that day, I watched God transform my life to center around Him. Going into high school, I knew I needed to surround myself with people who would help me maintain my faith. I knew I wanted to be happy. I knew I needed to step into a lifestyle that was centered around Jesus instead of just going to Him when it was convenient for me. I noticed my life change. Friendships changed. Relationships changed. The type of person I was changed. My confidence grew. I stepped out of my comfort zone and began letting God take control.

Just because I had Jesus didn't mean that my life was going to be perfect, but it did mean that I could get through anything because I had the all-powerful God on my side. Since then, I have focused every day on living out God's will for my life. While I am still trying to get things about me figured out, I have gained confidence in my identity. I have found that I have stopped stressing about things that don't matter, and I am more content and happier!

My anxieties have diminished significantly! While I do get anxious sometimes, my everyday anxieties have disappeared and my stomach issues are managed with diet and medicine. I began to shift my schedule to manage my stomach issues and give God the attention He deserved. Every morning I got up 45 minutes earlier and ate breakfast. I prepared my breakfast and sat down to read the Bible. By changing my schedule, I have not only improved my physical health but strengthened my spiritual health as well. I am doing better now than I have been in over five years.

Getting into the Word every day has changed my life. I take one verse from the chapter I read and I write it down on a sticky note, so I can keep it throughout the day. Along with living out my verse of the day, I listen mostly to Christian (with a sprinkle of country and a whole lotta Christmas) music. I have found that other music doesn't encourage and inspire me like Christian music does. It is *p-o-w-e-r-f-u-l* and instead of bad music getting stuck in my brain, I have truth turned into a tune all day long!

Now, I'm nowhere near perfect, but I learned that perspective is important. I also learned that God uses experiences to shape us into the person He created us to be, and we need to surround ourselves with people who support our walk with Him. Proverbs 13:20 says, "Walk with the wise and become wise; associate with fools and get in trouble" (NLT)9. Finding good, christian friends has been the best blessing in my life. Being surrounded with godliness allows my heart to stay on track, while still having fun. My friends now are the most amazing people who have influenced me and my decisions to continue living for Him.

"Walk with the wise and become wise; associate with fools and get in trouble."

Proverbs 13:20 (NLT)(9)

Acknowledgements

Thank you to my mom who encouraged me to use my writing ability to glorify God and write this book in the first place. This amazing lady spent countless hours reading my manuscript, analyzing the book structure, and processing the information that I wanted to include in this book. She's my hero, best friend, and biggest influence.

Thank you to my beautiful grandma who edited the entire book thoroughly. With her incredibly godly background, she solidified the biblical information and called me to discuss confusing lines or mistakes. I had so much fun working with her, and I am grateful that God used her English background to help me through this process. Her godly influence truly developed me as a Christian, and I'm thankful that God placed me in her family. Thank you to my grandpa who has encouraged and guided me along this process, as well. You and grandma were a huge part of every step in this book - even listening to my late night breakdown calls, oops! Love you guys so much!

Thank you to my cousin, Cory, for guiding me first through the marketing and business planning of my cupcake business when I was 12 years old and now influencing me to share what God has laid on my heart and publish a book! You have guided me through timelines, marketing plans, design ideas, publishing options, and the overall experience. You've shown me that you can step out of your comfort zone and succeed if you put your mind to it, and I'm forever grateful.

Thank you to my amazing dad for helping me find publishing options and talking through my decisions. You are my biggest godly influence, and I continue to learn from your faith every single day. Thank you for your unending support throughout this process! You are my biggest encourager, and I wouldn't be the person, or Christian, I am today without your love and guidance!

Thank you to my friend, Paige, for the cover photography. She's incredible, not only on the soccer field, but in picture angles and editing! Thank you for taking the time to make sure my cover picture was perfect!

Thank you to my friend, JT, for helping me a TON with pictures and editing. He has influenced me in so many ways, and I couldn't be more grateful to have him in my life. He has helped me with social media platforms, videography, photo editing, and color coordinating. Thank you for also always being willing to run or bike during any part of the day, for any crazy distance!

I want to give a HUGE thank you to my best friends! They have been nothing but loving and supporting throughout this whole process! To Clay, thank you for being my biggest supporter throughout this process. I'm so blessed to know you! To Eva, thank you for being such a huge part of my life. You have been there from the start, and I couldn't ask for a better best friend. To Beau, thank you for being such a godly influence in my life. God truly used you throughout my sanctification process, and you have led me on the godly path in all areas of my life. To Aariyah, thank you for the incredible support through this. You and your family have such a special place in my heart, and I am blessed to call you my best friend! Thank you for being my go-to adventure girl!

Lastly, I want to thank Cathie and Tyler Quillet who have made this all possible. Signing with your new company was the biggest God-led blessing I've ever experienced. Thank you for working with me to make this dream come true. Tyler, thank you for analyzing the manuscript and helping me with context and grammar. Thank you for helping me make my book come alive! Cathie, thank you for the cover design, interior designs, and advertisements! You have made my vision come to life, and I never imagined my book looking as amazing as it turned out! Thank you both for believing in me and answering God's call to start a publishing company. I remember looking up to both of you from a very young age, and I think it's incredible that our paths meet again!

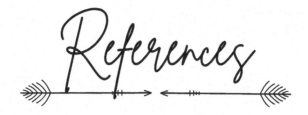

References

1. Curran, Sean. "Bigger Than I Thought." Bigger Than I Thought, sixstepsrecords. 2019, 5. Youtube, www.youtube.com/watch?v=o9YnFjsc2XY

2. Compiled & Edited by BST & Crosswalk Staff, BibleStudyTools Staff. "Judas Betrays Jesus - Bible Story." Biblestudytools.com, Salem Web Network, 20 July 2018, www.biblestudytools.com/bible-stories/judas-betrayed-jesus-bible-story.html.

3. MarkW. "The Role of the Queen Bee." PerfectBee, PerfectBee, 16 Sept. 2020, www.perfectbee.com/learn-about-bees/the-life-of-bees/role-queen-bee.

4. Powell-Lunder, Jennifer. "Understanding Why Queen Bees Are Able to Hold Court." Psychology Today, 2 Nov. 2013, www.psychologytoday.com/us/blog/lets-talk-tween/201311/understanding-why-queen-bees-are-able-hold-court.

5. "Friendship." Dictionary.com, Dictionary.com, 2020, www.dictionary.com/browse/friendship?s=t.

6. Chamblin, Knox J. "Godly, Godliness Definition and Meaning - Bible Dictionary." Biblestudytools.com, www.biblestudytools.com/dictionary/godly-godliness/.

7. Northwestern Medicine. "Five Benefits of Healthy Relationships." Northwestern Medicine, 2020, www.nm.org/healthbeat/healthy-tips/5-benefits-of-healthy-relationships.

8. PassionStudents. "DATING: Why Your Checklist Is Worthless - Ben Stuart." YouTube, YouTube, 5 Aug. 2017, www.youtube.com/watch?v=BjB8CUVA4_c.

9. Athlete's Bible: Let's Go Edition (FCA). NLT ed., Holman Bible Staff, Fellowship of Christian Athletes, 2019.

10. "John 15: ESV Bible: YouVersion." ESV Bible | YouVersion, www.bible.com/bible/59/JHN.15.ESV.

11. "Partnership." Dictionary.com, Dictionary.com, 2020, www.dictionary.com/browse/partnership.

12. Synonyms of Partner." www.thesaurus.com, 2020, www.thesaurus.com/browse/partner?s=t.

Made in USA - Kendallville, IN
86258_9798717321709
04.12.2023 1301